THE LITTLE BOOK OF
FISHING

A FISHING A to Z

Written by Rob Yorke with Greg Meenehan

THE LITTLE BOOK OF
FISHING

This edition first published in the UK in 2004
By Green Umbrella Publishing

© Green Umbrella Publishing 2008

www.gupublishing.co.uk

Publishers Jules Gammond and Vanessa Gardner

Printed and bound in China

ISBN-13: 978-0-954456-13-9
ISBN-10: 0-954456-13-0

Contents

Angling

ANGLING EVOKES IN ME EITHER A sense of joy or a feeling of frustration. I experience joy at being water side, seeing the view from a hillside lake, feeling the tug of a fish at the end of my line, or hearing the splash of a fish rising in the dark.

But I feel frustration when from my office or car I see another angler set foot for the water, encumbered with rod, bag and net. Maybe he, too, is aware of the ancient proverb that "the gods do not deduct from man's allotted span the hours spent in fishing".

One thing is for sure - we are not alone. Over four million coarse, sea and game anglers spend in excess of £3.3 billion in the UK pursuing a frequently illusive and often inedible quarry. But the largest participant sport in the UK remains something of a mystery to the non-angling public, who admit to bafflement when asked to account for the

attraction of the hobby. And even within the fishing community, coarse, sea and game anglers lead very separate lives.

Novelist John Buchan came close to the truth when he wrote "The charm of fishing is that it is the pursuit of what is elusive but attainable, a perpetual series of occasions for hope".

With 25,000 different species of fish in the world, and 78 per cent of the world covered in water (not including ice), the potential for catching a fish should be pretty good. Most anglers use rods, reels and line, though some in far off coun-

million years. The coelacanth was widespread in the world's oceans 350 million years ago (200 million years before the dinosaurs) and was still forming part of the diet of east African islanders 65 years ago.

Although this Little Book of Fishing will cover mainly rod and line, I have strayed into a couple of other related subjects. The main purpose of angling was once to get dinner on to the table, whether via ice-hole, rock pool or literally by hook or by crook. The supermarket and modern piscatorial practises have since divorced us from that basic necessity, but not from the prehistoric hunting instinct that afflicts anglers.

tries have been known to favour bows and arrows, and others in Japan even train birds to regurgitate their catch, while I as a young lad used my hands to tickle trout.

In many eyes, angling is a metaphor for life and the pursuit of happiness, so neglect at your peril the advice of an anglers' handbook published in 1805 that states "Thou shalt not fish in troubled water".

In 1938 fishermen in the Indian Ocean caught a species that the world had thought had been extinct for 60

OPPOSITE What Britain was made for!

BELOW The coelacanth was thriving some 350 million years ago

Use of stick and line by the earliest Egyptians in 2000 BC has evolved into implements of great fish-catching sophistication. The use of such a rod now necessitates the purchase of an Environment Agency licence for angling in the UK's freshwaters, and forms part of the most written-about pastime, recreation or sport in British literature. The telling of stories among the 'brethren of the angle' is as old as angling itself, and what the hobby loses in translation to television it more than makes up when consigned to the page.

Angling can be divided into three main branches of the sport, based on the fish being pursued, namely coarse, sea and game. They all have their own peculiarities, techniques, rods, reels and baits, but anglers of all three persuasions are united in agreement with the Roman poet Ovid that "Chance is always powerful. Let your hook be always cast: in the pool where you least expect there will be fish".

Sea anglers have the biggest 'pool' in which to cast with the possibility of catching one of the 350 species that swim around the UK coast. They are exposed to the elements on piers, rocky outcrops, sand and pebble beaches and

In writing this book I have substituted the word 'fishing' with 'angling' due to historic references to fishing with an angle (or fish hook) and Chambers Dictionary definition of 'angle' as "to fish with rod and line". Moreover, the term 'angler' conveniently removes the need for potentially sexist references to the fisherman!

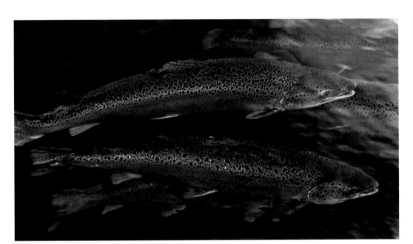

on board boats in the hope of bringing home something to feed the family.

From huge reservoirs to tiny tarns, king-size rivers to simple streams, game anglers pursue around five species amid some of the most spectacular scenery in Britain. Salmon are kings among game fish - the term 'game' indicating that they are edible. With an average chance of catching one estimated at one in every 5,000 casts, they are not for the faint hearted or impatient.

Coarse anglers are in the majority in Britain and have a varied selection of fish to try to catch, from razor-toothed pike to dainty dace, using a multitude of simple or sophisticated methods.

Codes of practise, fish care and bank-side etiquette are now prevalent in angling, to preserve the fish and the environment for future anglers. Perhaps increasingly anglers will borrow ideas from each other and benefit from lessons learned in pursuit of other species. Fly-fishing for pike, chub and bass is as much a joyous way to angle as spinning for salmon or worming for trout.

Angling has its fair share of snobbery, based on the skill needed to employ a tactic successfully, and the degree of handicap it embodies. Even the meekest form of angling can be guilty of 'high church' tendencies, where one technique is considered less sporting than another.

But the timeless attraction of angling is, as the founding father of angling literature Izaak Walton concluded, that it "may be said to be so much like the mathematics that it can never be fully learned". That is the joy of the sport - the puzzle is never completed. Whether it be hunting specimen carp, a keepnet full of tench in a match, a bucket of feather-caught mackerel, the thrill of a reel screaming with the pull of a first salmon, or simply the pleasure of striding over high, heathery hills with trout rod in hand in the hope of sport.

BELOW Coarse anglers are in the majority in Britain

Bait & Billingsgate

BAIT COMES BEFORE FISHING LIKE a horse comes before a cart. If you don't believe me, try going fishing and then looking for your bait!

As a young lad I felt the call of the stream, but first I had to find my worm. If the weather had been hot, the usual turning over of big stones in the corner of the garden yielded nothing, and the forking over of the smelly manure heap revealed only the tails of fast-disappearing worms. It was always a relief to snare my prize – often a big, fat brandling.

There are 27 species of earthworm in the UK, and there are anglers who are organised enough to 'grow' their own in wormeries of moist moss or shredded newspaper, kept cold on the stone of the garage floor.

Perch love worms and are not fussy as to how they are presented. I was once forced to improvise, having forgotten my rod in all the excitement. I cut a hazel twig and tied on nylon and a hook, then made a float from a piece of reed. Carefully I threaded the worm on to the hook to prevent the perch from stealing it, and was rewarded with a decidedly indignant 'footballer' in his striped jersey.

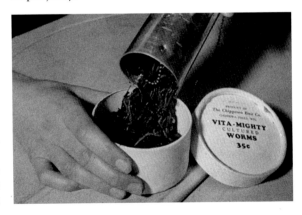

BELOW Worms have been used as bait for centuries

Bream are also fond of worms, in particular small redworms, but are fonder still of a 'cocktail' combination of a worm sitting on a hook alongside a single, red-coloured maggot.

Sea anglers also use worms, the seafaring equivalent of the earthworm being lugworm and ragworm, both of which require a deal more work to extract them from their underground homes. There are dangers involved, too! The king ragworm can grow up to two feet in length and has extendable jaws, while the yellowtail lugworm emits iodine when threaded on a hook, which stains the hands bright yellow.

Flatfish are big fans of ragworm, in particular when it is hooked on the tip of the hook in combination with another bait, to add motion and an irresistible scent.

Other sea fish baits include limpets, mussels, peeler crabs, sandeels, squid, razorfish and the worthy mackerel.

Most baits are best when fresh, as fish hunt mainly by smell. If you are fishing for big fish such as conger eel, halibut or shark, a whole mackerel or one sliced at the end to flutter attractively in the tide is the perfect bait for these hungry beasts.

Bread crust is one of the simplest and cheapest baits available, and one with almost universal appeal. Most coarse fish will eat it, as will trout, and so will sea fish such as mullet. Carp fishing with crust cast on to the surface of the water is an art in itself, requiring, stealth, cunning and plenty of free offerings, but well worth the sacrifice of your sandwiches.

Hempseed was once believed to hold a narcotic attraction for fish, being the seed of the cannabis plant, though others believe fish take the tiny dark shells for freshwater snails.

Hardly a single garden creature or supermarket product has escaped the attention of anglers in search of bait. From slugs and wasp grubs to cheese and marshmallows, all have done time on the end of a line.

Few modern carp anglers will venture out without 'boilies', which are made from milk protein powder mixed with eggs and dunked in boiling water until they form a skin that makes them impregnable to small fish. These marble-size balls are made in a million different colours and flavours, and carp love 'em, as do barbel, tench and chub. Microwaving them instead of boiling them makes them float, allowing anglers to anchor them just off the lake bed, threaded on a 'hair' of light line tied to the hook.

BELOW A selection of multi-coloured boilies

Billingsgate

BILLINGSGATE IS THE PLACE FOR fresh fish. The UK's biggest inland fish market, in Lower Thames Street, East London, shifts on average 25,000 tonnes of fish and fish products every year. At 5.30am you will hear stallholders bidding for business – "Lovely Dover Soles at £5.23 a lb; beautiful pink salmon at 95p per lb; wild salmon from the Highlands at £10 a lb; turbot at £7.50 a lb; cod at £2.11 a lb; or some loverly fresh eels at £3.50 a lb".

The present market is "a free and open market for all sorts of fish whatsoever" as set out in an Act of Parliament in 1699. The original market was set up in 1327 under rights granted by Edward III that prohibited the setting up of rival markets within 6.6 miles of the City –

BELOW Early morning activity at a thriving Billingsgate

ABOVE Farm-fished bass awaiting distribution at Billingsgate

the distance a person could be expected to walk to market, sell produce and return in one day.

Billingsgate was originally a market for corn, iron, wine, salt and pottery as well as for fish, and did not become associated exclusively with fish until the 16th Century, its present listed building being opened in 1876.

By 8am the action is all over for the day at Billingsgate, deliveries having been arriving throughout the night from every fishing port in the UK, from Penzance to Aberdeen. Modern technology means fish is imported frozen on refrigerator ships or flown-in chilled, and this accounts for 40 per cent of business.

Farmed fish are much in evidence, with species such as turbot, cod and bass joining salmon on the production line in Scotland, Norway and across Europe. With gloomy predictions about natural sea fish stocks and a constant call for conservation, these farmed fish will start to play a more important role in our continuing desire to eat fresh fish.

Carp, Char & Cod

CARP ARE PART OF ONE OF THE biggest families of coarse fish in freshwater – the cyprinids. The cyprinidae grouping includes goldfish, barbel, bream, chub, tench and roach.

Common carp came to England from the continent in the Middle Ages, transported in boats while wrapped in wet sacks. Monks kept these 'wildies' in ponds at monasteries, to provide food on holy days, when they abstained from eating meat.

Three types of carp interest the modern carp angler – mirror carp (with few scales), common carp (fully scaled) and leather carp (with no scales), all of which grow to over 50 lb, can live for 50 years and have earned themselves individual nicknames.

Crucian carp are a golden, hand-size species with a bizarre habit of swimming in circles when hooked. Many have interbred with common carp and goldfish to create hybrids. The presence of barbules at the corners of the mouth is a dead giveaway.

Ornamental varieties such as fantail carp, blue carp, koi and ghost carp are now caught regularly, along with grass carp and F1 crucian or goldfish-based carp hybrids, which are 'designer' fish engineered not to increase in size above 3 lb.

In Tudor times a stuffed mirror carp would have been the centrepiece of a banquet in England, and in the Czech

Republic it was a popular choice for Christmas dinner. Fishmongers here still sell them, but woe betide anyone who tries to take home Lumpy, Stumpy or Stumpy's Mate for Sunday lunch!

Carp are found in rivers and canals, with fish in the River Thames and the Grand Union Canal reaching an impressive size, but lakes are the most popular and prolific venues.

The modern emphasis is on cleverly designed end-tackle to outwit the biggest and wariest fish. Such was the respect accorded to carp that when arguably the greatest angler of all time, Richard Walker, landed his British record carp of 44 lb in 1952 at Redmire Pool, in Herefordshire, the species was considered by many almost too cunning to catch.

Angling traditionalist Chris Yates took the record to a new height with a 51 lb 8 oz mirror carp from the same water in 1980 using a 25-year-old split-cane rod - made, coincidentally by Richard Walker - and an equally old Ambidex reel. And the record has since broken the 60 lb barrier, thanks to climate change and a rich diet of anglers' high-protein baits.

Char

CHAR (OR CHARR) are one of Britain's most beautiful and mysterious game fish. Their status as a game fish is confirmed by the presence of an adipose fin – the tiny protrusion found on the fish's back between its dorsal fin and tail.

Char have a number of subgroups, not all of which have been classified yet, and originate from migratory arctic char. For all the red, green and gold beauty of the char, one would assume that it lives in the sparkling upper surface of the water, but it is a fish that lives at great depth. One Scottish char was reported recently as having been

ABOVE Chris Yates' record-breaking 51lb 8oz mirror carp

LEFT Carp is still the traditional Czech Christmas dish

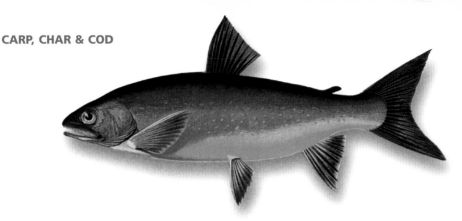

brought up from 500 ft below the surface of Loch Ness.

Mrs Beeton reckoned that the char was one of the best tasting fish ever to swim, better even than salmon, with its rich, red flesh full of fat, making it perfect to pot and preserve for a rainy day.

And rainy days there are a-plenty where char reside. Scotland and northern England hold the UK's char stocks, where they are able to survive in the vast depths, since the temperature and the oxygen levels are to their liking.

Special techniques and equipment have been designed down the years to reap the harvest of char, from fly fishing in Loch Doon to deep trailing with rigs in Lake Windermere and using downriggers in Ireland's Lough Mask.

Traditional Windermere hand-made char fishing tackle has been around for 170 years and is employed by hanging a heavy weight at a depth of 25 metres, from which trail up to eight tiny spinners. These slivers of bright metal are trailed from the boat at about one and a half miles per hour to imitate the small fish on which the char prey. Storing and using a char fishing rig is a skilled business if horrendous tangles are not to ensue, and the depth at which they fish mean the char fisherman can expect to net only three out of every five fish that fall for his spinners.

Char do not grow very big, the average being a pan-size 8 oz to 12 oz, but these deep trailing expeditions have yielded much bigger fish, most notably ferox (cannibalistic) trout and pike, which can wreak havoc with the char tackle while creating a great deal of excitement in the boat!

Cod

COD HAVE BEEN SUPPLYING MAN with sea food in the northern hemisphere for up to 1,000 years, and have inspired culinary protestations of love.

Chef Alain Senderens proclaims "The cod is so beautiful, the way the flesh unfolds in white leaves", but the fish's great eating qualities have proved its undoing, with talk of possible extinction.

The cod family is made up of many species, including haddock and whiting, but is also one of the hardiest of fishes, carrying as it does its own form of antifreeze to counteract the frozen arctic seas it frequents.

Catholic in its tastes, it is prepared to eat almost anything, and often does. Among the items recently discovered in the stomachs of cod are a man's head (in a 97 lb Morgan cod caught off Australia), a letter (still legible) and an unopened can of Coca-Cola!

Cod are among the most prolific of egg producers, with one specimen recording 9.1 million eggs, making them seemingly ideal candidates for farm rearing now that stocks in the North Sea and the north Atlantic have been plundered to dangerously low levels.

Whether Mrs Beeton and her 17 recipes for cod had anything to do with this cod-lust we may never know. What we do know is that she wasted nothing, serving up the head and tongue as dainty delicacies.

Cod favour deep-water locations, in particular around sunken wrecks, but are also caught from the shore. The British boat-caught record weighed 58 lb 6 oz and came out to Noel Cook fishing off Whitby in 1992, while the shore-caught record stands at 44 lb 8 oz, caught from Barry, in South Wales.

Scotland and the Isle of Wight are renowned for their cod fishing, with rough seas in winter emboldening the fish to feed close in shore for the worms turned up by the waves. Boat anglers favour squid or crab, or a shiny weighted piece of metal called a pirk jerked up and down over a wreck. Anglers who make their own have been known to catch cod on old door handles, chair legs and spanners with big treble hooks attached.

BELOW A brace of boat-caught cod

Dogfish & Dapping

RIGHT The lesser spotted dogfish would win no prizes in a beauty contest

BELOW The bull huss (or greater spotted dogfish) is a loner

DOGFISH ARE THE UGLY FISH OF the sea. Their image is so poor and unfashionable that they need a pseudonym before they can be eaten. I know a fine fish-and-chip shop in west London that sells delicious rock salmon (alias dogfish) at the same price as cod. Huss is now the official name for dogfish, which command a good price at Billingsgate.

The early explorers of the Americas were among the first to feast on the bellies of dogfish, having recognised its fine culinary attributes. In the 1990s America renamed dogfish 'Cape shark' to export it in vast quantities to Asia. This re-branding is closer to its true identity than the 'rock salmon' tag, since dogfish are a member of the shark family. But their looks have been their undoing and many anglers are less than pleased to see them.

Both species have very abrasive sandpaper-like skin that can give the unwary angler a sore arm if the tail is allowed to wrap around during unhooking. But their skeleton has no bones, only cartilage, so they can be held harmlessly by bringing the tail up to join the head.

Dogfish have poor eyesight, and so hunt mainly by smell, carrying a bait away rather like a dog. Almost any bait will catch them, but two or three strikes may be needed to set the hook.

Market stalls in northern France are full of dogfish, which are a popular meal, yet the British have never taken to them, despite the threat to other sea species caused by overfishing.

Maybe if we knew more about them we could learn to love them more. Dogfish don't lay eggs like other fish but take two years to give birth to between five and ten perfect pups. A little more respect to the doggie, please!

BELOW Smoothhounds are the biggest and best fighters of the dogfish family

The dogfish family consists of a number of species, all known collectively as 'doggies', with the smoothhound being the largest and best fighter. Although it looks like shark-look-alike the tope, the smoothhound has no sharp incisors but flat, grinding teeth to crunch up crabs and worms it finds while patrolling the sea bottom.

The bull huss (or greater spotted dogfish) is a loner and lives in deep water, whereas the lesser spotted dogfish likes to live in shallow water. The collective noun for a shoal of dogfish is a 'troop'.

Dapping

DAPPING WAS PROBABLY ONE OF the earliest forms of fly-fishing and involves dangling a fly, real or artificial, over the water from an overhanging bank or from a boat. Chub will respond well to a large bushy fly dapped gently on the surface of a river, mistaking it for a quivering, wind blown moth or an upturned beetle as they rise, tentatively, to suck in the offering.

ABOVE Irish loughs like Mask have a long tradition of dapping

The hallowed turf of the River Test, in Hampshire, England's premier trout chalkstream, used to have a large number of big chub which were caught by skilled anglers using appropriate artificial flies, the larger and rougher the better. These fish were then removed to other waters to provide more room for the more highly valued trout.

But the real place to dap is from a traditional boat on an Irish lough in search of vividly marked natural brown trout during the mayfly season. Between May and June on certain limestone lakes and rivers, the water comes alive with mayflies hatching on every inch of the water's surface, and trout gorging themselves to excess.

Mayflies live for only 24 hours after hatching, having ascended from the river bed where they waited patiently as a nymph for their moment of glory. Anglers can either use an artificial fly or capture the flighted adults alive and secure them to a hook for dapping.

No casting is required for this form of angling, as the long rods used are fitted with floss blow-lines, which billow in the breeze, pushing the fly out over the water in front of the drifting boat.

Patience, concentration and sharp eyesight are needed, because the excitement of the sudden, splashy rise after a period of inactivity is almost too much to behold, and a mistimed strike can result in failure.

The biggest fish often fall to the dapped fly, appearing out of the depths and executing a slow-motion head-and-tail roll over it. You must wait for the fish to turn down with its prize before striking, or the hook will be pulled from its mouth.

At other times you will drift into a reverie looking at the spectacular view or a golden eagle soaring overhead, when suddenly you are rudely awakened by an almighty splash as an enormous tail of a disappearing trout waves goodbye to your opportunity.

Sea-trout are great takers of the dapped flies, in particular the Loch Ordie and the Soldier Palmer, but they prefer them fished more actively, by sending them skimming and skittering across the surface in front of the boat. Sea-trout are migratory and (like salmon) don't feed in fresh water, but take the fly because they resent its presence on the surface. They seem to strike out in annoyance at it, or perhaps they are responding to some involuntary reflex reaction honed in their sea-feeding days.

Other anglers may not like to be cooped up in a boat, and take the action to the bank. In a strong gale, when you'd rather not be tossed around on a lough, you can wade into the edge of the lake and dap a large fly across the water, close to the bank. Trout that have come into the shallows to feed on the disturbed lake bottom will rise at your fly in spectacular fashion, and chase it across the surface. I have taken good rainbow trout on a large fly cast across

ABOVE Mayflies live for only 24 hours after hatching

the rolling waves and dapped back across the surface of the breakers. In windy weather, though, I would advise the wearing of glasses to protect your eyes from wind-borne hooks.

Ernest Hemingway knew the attraction of dapping. In The Big Two-Hearted River he tells a wonderfully evocative short story about an angler camping in the wilds who collects grasshoppers, threads them on a hook and wades into an icy stream. He daps the hopper down the river and hooks, but then loses, a monster trout. "Nick's hand was shaky. He reeled in slowly. The thrill had been too much." Stirring stuff.

Eel

RIGHT Fish baits work well for freshwater eels

ABOVE Sandeels (or launce) make an excellent bait for several species

EELS ARE EXTRAORDINARY FISH. They have the ability to survive out of water, to breed in a sea that is thousands of miles away, to live up to 40 years old, and to tangle lines unmercifully and irredeemably.

Reviled by many anglers but eaten with relish (literally) by lots of Londoners, they are loved and hated in equal measure. When smoked they are mouth-wateringly tasty, but while jellied eels may not be everyone's cup of tea, the Ancient Greeks called the eel the king of fish, and those who caught them were excused from paying taxes.

All freshwater eels in the UK start life in the Sargasso Sea, near the Gulf of Mexico. The newly born eel, in its leaf-like form known as a leptocephalus, drifts in the Gulf Stream for up to three years, gradually growing into an elver and appearing in UK rivers in April.

Spring high tides help elvers run the rivers, and these tides can cause mini tidal waves, such as the Severn Bore, to course up estuaries and along rivers, aiding the eels' ascent.

Thousands make the migration, and licensed fisherman congregate on the shores to net the tiny elvers for market, mainly on the continent, with prices per kilogram higher than gold.

Eels sport different colours at different ages, which once convinced many people that there were two different species. Mystery surrounds the eel's methods of reproduction, and this brought strange reflections from certain

Any meat, fish or worm will succeed in catching an eel, but the best time to fish for them is at night. One of the most inventive methods ever devised involves filling a sack with offal and balls of wool and leaving it in the water overnight. In the morning you can marvel at how the eels have entered the bag and become caught in the offal-infused wool, their backward-slanting teeth preventing their escape.

An adaptation of this technique for rod-and-line fishing without a hook is known as babbing. This involves

BELOW Eels can be a handful even on the bank

observers. The Greek philosopher Pliny thought that eels managed to self-procreate by rubbing themselves against rocks, while Izaak Walton thought that eels appeared from within rotten planks and out of the dewy grasses and mud. It was not until 1921 that a mid-Atlantic catch discovered that all eels actually originate in the Sargasso Sea.

Catching eels is fairly straightforward. I last caught one in a cold mountain stream in Corsica on a piece of salami commandeered from my sandwich. This eel wanted my bait so much that it was not put off by my jumping in and swimming in the pool.

ABOVE Conger eels can grow even bigger than this 72 lb fish

who has landed an eel only to have it escape and make its way back to the water. There are eyewitness accounts of eels crossing wet fields on damp, moonless nights on their migratory route back to the sea.

Herons are particularly partial to eels, and will stake-out any ditches being dredged by diggers, to feast on the unfortunate eels as they are dumped on the bank in a mound of stinking mud.

At the other end of the scale, the unrelated conger eel lives in rock crevices or ship-wrecks in the sea and is very secretive in its habits. It can reach over 100 lb in weight, and can be tempted by a bloody bait such as mackerel head and guts on a sharp hook, a wire trace and a strong line.

Landing a conger is another matter, however. They fight tenaciously and will wrap their tail around the structure of their home if allowed to get back in their lair.

Once in the boat the fight is not over. Their powerful jaws and razor-sharp teeth are said to be capable of biting through fingers like fudge, and still retain their closing reflex after death, as anglers foolish enough to toy with their

threading wool through a worm with a needle, tying the wool to a line and lowering it from the end of a rod into the water. The wool's teeth-snagging properties do the job of a hook.

The presence of eels in land-locked waters suggests they are able to travel overland, a fact borne out by anyone

catch have found to their cost.

Conger spawn only once in their lifetime, in deep water near Madeira, and produce up to 15 million eggs. The lifecycle is similar to that of the freshwater eel, the eggs drifting with sea currents until they arrive in UK waters and set up home in suitable lairs.

There are those who say that conger will bark when brought out of the water. I once saw television chef Rick Stein meet a character whose dog was trained to 'sniff out' conger at low tide by barking at them!

Sandeels (or launce), however, are more preyed upon than predator, being small and living, as their name suggests, under or on sandy sea beds. Fish and birds are equally fond of them, and the presence of sandeels will usually indicate big fish. As soon as I catch a sea-trout stuffed to the gills with sandeels I change to a artificial fly made to look like an eel, with an immediate response. Sandeels are used as bait for a number of sea fish species, and can even be used live for bass and turbot.

I end this chapter with a plea for conservation when it comes to freshwater eels. Once common, they are now severely threatened, with the European population recently said to be currently just one per cent of its 1980 level.

There is no more cautionary tale than that of the eel pout or burbot – once so prolific that it was netted and spread on fields as fertiliser in eastern England. Then in the 1960 it was discovered that there were few left, and in the 1970s a cash incentive was offered as a desperate incentive for someone to track down a last, undisturbed colony in some untouched backwater. Alas, no-one came forward to claim the prize, and it is now widely accepted that the once prolific eel pout has gone the way of the dodo and the passenger pigeon into extinction.

This sad-looking fish which was considered a delicacy, and achieved the accolade of appearing in both the first written description of fishing in the English language and in a Chekov play, is now no more. Take heed, and take care of the eel, this most misunderstood of fishes, whether you love them or loathe them, for what once is lost can never be restored.

BELOW Burbot like this one in the bottom case were once prolific

Fly & Float

FLY-FISHING IS THE ULTIMATE con-trick – the outwitting of a fish without recourse to offering anything that is genuinely edible. The finest fly-fishers also tie their own flies, combining two equally engrossing sides of the hobby to achieve supreme satisfaction and the ultimate accolade – a double endorsement of your skills by the fish you were trying to catch.

The Romans began fly-fishing by winding red wool around their hooks and fastening them to the feathers that grow under a cock's wattles, while in the Middle Ages Germans fished for trout and grayling using a feathered hook.

The first English book on fly-fishing was written by Dame Juliana Berners in 1496. Treatyse of Fysshynge wyth an Angle, to give it its proper title, contained a wealth of practical angling advice on new equipment, such as rods made with braided horsetails tied to their tips. Reels had not arrived yet, and given the limitations of the equipment, it is unlikely that anglers in the 15th Century used lines longer than twice the length of their rods.

This set-up would probably have worked out just as effective as trying to punch 40 metres of forward-tapered line into a breeze, but fly-fishing anglers in those days probably intentionally deposited the line on the water and allowed the wind to move the flies. One sharp angler of that era noted that it was wise to pick a windy and dark afternoon, but added the recommendation to stay away from trees!

It was Izaak Walton, albeit a worm angler at heart, who, in his angling tome The Compleat Angler, published in 1653, breathed life and soul into the art of fly-fishing. Even though anglers were now using 20 ft rods, his basic principle of fly-casting still applies. It involves the use of a rod moved backwards and forwards as an extension of the arm to project a weighted line, tipped with a leader to which a fly is attached, on to the water.

Technology has made fly rods lighter than ever, and there are now as many ways of fly-fishing as there are methods for catching roach, carp and pike. Dry-fly fishing for trout employs a close imitation of a natural insect, and requires a fair amount of experience and skill. You need to land a fly without disturbance on to the nose of a wild fish feeding on natural flies, then tempt it and hook it. Identifying the food on which the fish is feeding is

OPPOSITE Fly-fishing for stocked trout takes place on purpose-made lakes

LEFT Fly casting is a skill well worth learning

ABOVE Grayling take a fly on rivers like this one in Wales

instance, if a big, gaudy fly is to be cast to a salmon lying in a fast, deep pool at the start of the season in February, an ultra-fast lead-core sinking line could be required.

Fly-fishing on purpose-made lakes stocked with sizeable brown and rainbow trout is very popular, and on large reservoirs, boats can be hired or long-casting shooting-head fly lines employed to throw huge distances across these waters while the angler stands, heron-like, in the margins.

also part of that skill, as is finding the ideal place to cast.

Wet-fly fishing involves the use of flies or lures cast on to the water and then retrieved back under the water, either to simulate fry (young fish) or insects, or to stimulate the fish's predatory instincts. Trout are certainly predatory. I was fishing a wet fly on a tiny Welsh lake when I hooked a small brown trout which was already stuffed with four baby newts!

The skill of wet-fly fishing is to present the fly with its most natural motion, and much depends on water temperature and your choice of quarry. The fly line is responsible for presenting the fly at different depths, whether floating, slow sinking or fast sinking. For

Float

FLOAT FISHING BRINGS A WHOLE new meaning to the word 'concentration'. The crucial indicator that a fish has taken your bait and that you must strike if you are to have a chance of landing it, is a slim piece of painted wood.

Mr Sheringham summed it up perfectly in 1905 when he said "the float is pleasing in appearance and even more pleasing in disappearance". Float fishing can be undertaken with almost any type of coarse or sea rod and a fixed-spool reel, but the longer the rod the better will be your control of the float.

The float has many more uses than as a bite indicator. It suspends the bait at the preferred depth, carries the bait on the current or wind to an inaccessible location, and acts as a weight to facilitate casting the bait.

The slimmer the float the smaller the resistance felt by the sensitive mouth of a wary fish, and the smaller the amount of tip showing above the water, the earlier the angler is aware of a bite and more likely to succeed with the strike.

There are many variations on float construction – from wagglers, zoomers, sliders and quills to Avons, duckers, balsas and dibbers. All do a different job, and all have their day when conditions dictate that a certain combination is best for success.

Pole floats such as dibbers are among the smallest of floats and are suspended directly under poles attached on a fixed line to the tip of the pole via a length of elastic that extends when a fish is hooked.

Modern floats use a combination of natural and man-made materials, from balsa, cane, cork and elder pith to polystyrene, plastic, wire and carbon. Balsa wood is very buoyant but strong and

can be fashioned into almost any shape with sandpaper, and the shape of a float's body affects the way it sits in the water and behaves when the line is 'mended' or lifted off the surface to remove any slack.

Successful float fishing starts with plumbing the depth to discover the contours of the lake or river bed and to ensure that the bait is being fished close to or on the bottom. GPS technology has now made it possible to find the bottom and the fish with an electronic aid, with the arrival of the first wrist-mounted fish finder, but where's the skill (and fun) in that?

Trotting a float involves allowing the

BELOW Floats were once fashioned from cork and quills

river's flow to carry the bait to the fish, and the skill is to achieve such a degree of tackle control that your baited hook arrives among the fish in a way that is entirely natural, and matches that of the free offerings accompanying it down the river.

Another technique is stret-pegging, in which the bait and shot drag on the bed of a fast-flowing river, and the float is used to move the bait downstream at intervals. Fish love to hang out where there is a change in current speed or variance in depth, and this technique can be used as successfully for game fish, such as salmon (where bait fishing is allowed) as for coarse species.

Mackerel, garfish and mullet are all caught regularly by sea anglers fishing floats, in particular from piers and jetties or rocks, where a vantage point gives access to deep water. The great advantage of float fishing in these places is that the depth at which the bait is fishing can be varied throughout the day as the fish change depths with the conditions, simply by repositioning the float on the line. And if the area to be fished has a snaggy bottom, the tackle can be kept clear of these obstructions.

If you see a garfish near the surface,

reel in slowly and agitate the squid strip or ragworm in front of it, and wait for the thin-snouted garfish to get the morsel into its 'beak'. And if a live sandeel is hooked in the lip and lowered into the depths, the take you may get from a bass that follows it up from the bottom is likely to be savage.

RIGHT Modern plastic floats work very well for coarse and sea fishing

Gwyniad, Gudgeon, Grayling & Groundbait

Schelly record goes again

2 MAY 1976

...swater, in the Lake ...trict, has produced ...yet another record ...ally. The fish in our ...ure was caught by ...ally Wainwright of ...Helens and weighs ...2 lb—well over the present 1 lb 7½ oz record. It took a ...ed worm intended ...r trout and follows ...he capture of a 1 lb ...fish from the same ...ter two weeks ago by Peter Bromley.

GWYNIAD IS A LITTLE KNOWN fish found only in the depths of Lake Bala, in north Wales, that country's largest natural lake. It is the Welsh version of a freshwater houting, which form part of the whitefishes - a random collection of obscure game fish. How do we know they are related to salmon, char, trout and grayling? The presence of the adipose fin, which is a characteristic of Salmonidae.

How little we know of some of the fish that swim in our lakes. The fact that they are considered to be rare is based more on their secretive nature than on any grave threat to their populations.

They are protected in the UK, but in central and eastern Europe the freshwater

LEFT Relative of the gwyniad, the schelly is found in Ullswater

houting is of great economic significance, having been introduced into ponds as an auxiliary species to carp, though primarily as a food source.

Whitefishes in the UK are very localised, and each has its own name. The houting family consist of gwyniad, found in Lake Bala, powan, found in Loch Lomond, and Lough Eck, and skelly (or schelly) found in Ullswater. All three are very silvery, and so herring-like that some believed they were landlocked kippers.

Vendace and pollan are other species of whitefish found in very specific locations. Mill Loch in Dumfries once had a vendace club that would meet to net and feast on vendace. Their gradual drop in numbers was put down to the eutrophication of the lake from nutrient-rich surrounding land, rather than the netting. Game fish such as vendace and trout are generally more suited to oligotrophic waters (low in dissolved nutrients) than eutrophic waters (rich in nutrients), which suit coarse fish such as roach and bream better.

Gudgeon

GUDGEON ARE THE SMALL FRY OF the fish world, with a weight that rarely tops 4 oz. Yet for all its size it has a loyal following, and has attracted an extraordinary number of literary references over the years.

Angling for the gudgeon (Gobio gobio), which looks like a small barbel and is affectionately known as a 'gonk', was one of the coolest things to be seen doing in Victorian society, despite the fact that they were easy to catch. According to literature of the time, you had only to rake the river bed and they would come running.

As such, their name took on a double meaning in the dictionary as a derogatory term to describe one who is gullible and ready to swallow anything.

Grayling

GRAYLING ARE AN ALTOGETHER more wily fish, and carry with them a slightly mysterious air. They are a game fish, but they like to hang out with coarse fish in slower, eddying backwaters of rivers.

Their intolerance to pollution means they are a good indicator of the cleanliness of a river, as are minnows.

Pursued with vigour by anglers of all persuasions, grayling can be caught on both flies or bait, with maggots trotted down the current a favourite method, in particular on the coldest of autumn and winter days, when other fish refuse to feed.

The dorsal fin of the grayling (see previous page) is its most distinctive characteristic (followed by its natural odour of thyme and cucumber). It uses

BELOW Victorian society held the humble gudgeon in high esteem

Groundbait

GROUNDBAIT IS TO FISH WHAT the smell of fried bacon or fish and chips is to a hungry angler. The idea is to scatter finely ground crumbs of bread or cereal mixed with water to attract fish into the area of your hook bait.

A few samples of the same bait being used on the hook may also be mixed in, but the intention is to draw fish without feeding them up.

The use of groundbaiting devices was mentioned in The Practical Angler in 1842, where an implement with a small box full of holes was described. It would be stuffed with worms, which squirmed slowly out on to the bed of the lake or river.

The activity generated by a few feeding fish would attract others to come and claim part of the action, and this keenness not to miss out would allow fish to be hooked and extracted from the shoal without the others taking fright. The modern versions of these contraptions are known as swimfeeders, and they can be bought in a range of types and designs or made at home using lengths of plastic piping.

this fin when hooked to increase the force that the current is exerting on its body, turning sideways across the flow. Even small fish feel as if they are several times their weight when hooked in fast-moving water.

Predatory species such as pike and perch are not usually attracted by offering of bread groundbait, but the smaller species, such as bleak and minnows, which gather round will attract their attention. Also, groundbait can be used to take small, nuisance fish away, to allow something bigger to get a look-in. Pieces of bread thrown in and allowed to drift in the current will keep small fish absorbed for hours.

Sea anglers also use groundbait. A typical 'recipe' would consist of 80 per cent chopped fish and shellfish, 15 per cent bran (to bind it together) and a good splash of pilchard oil (for smell).

Groundbaiting will work from a pier, rocky outcrop, in an estuary or in a harbour. Conger eels are the Al Pacinos of the fish world, and will venture to see what's happening if there's a good bloodbath going on. And groundbaiting with breadcrust for grey mullet, as they cruise the shallows in estuaries and around piers, will pay dividends when you float out your baited crumb.

Chub are suckers for a trail of pieces of floating crust, brought to them by the current, and barbel have been known to be so keen to get at groundbait that they will pick up a swim-feeder and suck out the contents.

One of the deadliest ways of catching carp on day ticket waters is to mould fine groundbait round a specially shaped Method swimfeeder with the hookbait hidden inside. A carp will suck the groundbait in and give you a rod-bending bite.

Whether you buy special flavoured groundbait mixes or make your own by whizzing stale bread slices in the liquidiser, the principle of groundbaiting remains the same, and it remains a great way to boost your catches.

BELOW Plastic swimfeeders deposit groundbait alongside your hookbait

Hook &
Halibut

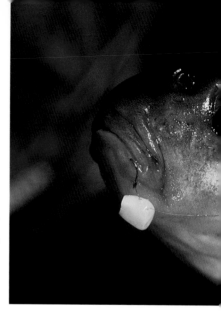

HOOKS ARE THE MOST IMPORTANT item in an angler's amoury. Their arrival marked the transition in man's hunting technique from brawn to brains, with the use of subtlety instead of strength.

Out went spears, harpoons and bare hands, and in came patience, guile and watercraft, with the result that the angler caught more and didn't have to get wet.

The first hooks were made of bone, and a metal one dated at 2,500 years of age has been found in the River Thames. Modern hooks are made from tempered carbon steel and have chemically etched points and anti-rust coatings, but the principle remains the same. The only refinements in design reflect the angler's increased knowledge of what works when and why.

Now you can choose from fine-wire, forged, reversed, offset, round-bend, wide-gape, crystal-bend, up-eyed, down-eyed, straight-eyed, spade-end, bronze, gilt, silvered, red or tungsten, in doubles, trebles or keel hooks, not to mention barbed, barbless or pinch barbless (half way between).

The addition of a barb to hooks has probably done more damage to anglers than it has to fish, which could be why one of the country's largest fishing

one for fish, though the anti-angling lobby would doubtless wish to disagree.

One of the commandments from the Anglers Handbook in 1805 states that "thou shalt not take small fish with large hooks". However, some species, such as salmon parr and small trout, run suicide missions, grabbing oversize hooks as if they wish to be caught.

Hook size is usually matched to the size of the fish being pursued. Sea hooks range in size from 6 up to 10/0, to deal with everything from dabs and flounders to cod and conger. However in freshwater angling, a tiny hook can

BELOW A wide variety of different types of hook is available

providers will not allow anglers to use anything else. Fish are very sensitive to what they put into their mouth, and the greater pressure needed to set a barbed hook in means there is less chance of catching it.

Many anglers prefer barbless hooks, both for the ease of hooking and ease of hook removal. But whichever you use, the same fish are caught again and again, and their keenness to swim away from the direction of the pull, rather than swim towards it, as you or I would if we were hooked, does appear to suggest that the experience is not a painful

often be used to outwit a huge fish, and with careful playing, a big chub or carp can be subdued on a size 20. This is usually when a big fish is hooked by accident, or conditions dictate that light tackle must be used, and it is considered more sporting to use tackle better suited to the job.

Waving a sharp piece of metal around all day inevitably leads to accidents, and most anglers have suffered at some stage in their fishing career. Hats with broad brims and sunglasses reduce the risk of getting a hook in the face. If you do fall victim, a pair of wire cutters is often a boon, for a hook can be pushed through more easily than it can be pulled out.

Second only in importance to the hook is the knot you use to attach it to your line. In the old days gut was used as the main line. I have a set of old salmon flies with catgut eyes whipped into the body of the fly. How that could hold a large salmon I can't imagine, but maybe standards of workmanship were much higher then.

Originally, hooks had spade-ends for connection to the leader. The Scottish invention of eyed hooks was a revelation, though many coarse anglers still use spade-end hooks because they say they make the bait sit more naturally in the water.

BELOW Treble hooks are used on spinners and for pike traces

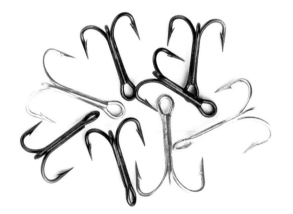

Halibut

HALIBUT CAN BE HUMONGOUS and are blessed with an appropriate Latin name of Hippoglossus hippoglossus. Some of the biggest rod-caught specimens have reached over 230 lb, and require a full harness for the rod butt to winch them up from the depths.

Rare and solitary bottom feeders, halibut are usually found between 50 and

300 metres down. A whole dead or live fish mounted on a large hook is used to catch them, and their much-prized flesh has a delicate, creamy flavour. They also make fine sushi.

Unlike halibut, other species of flatfish can be caught from the shore or from dinghies, using either a paternoster rig or a baited spoon. The latter has a flashy metal attractor like the bowl of a teaspoon attached about an inch above the ragworm-baited hook, and when the angler skims this across the seabed, it gives the impression of a smaller flatfish making off with a worm, which no big flounder likes to see happen.

Plaice are inquisitive and like the addition of coloured beads on the line, the brighter the better. Many 'flatties' prefer a cocktail bait such as lugworm tipped with squid or crab to a single offering.

Turbot are a prized catch, being very expensive to buy. They lie in ambush on off-shore banks waiting to use their tiny razor teeth on passing fish or sandeels.

All flatfish make good eating. Dover sole, sometimes called 'slips' or 'tongues', got their name from being transported from Kent to London for

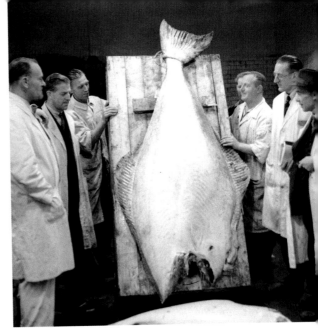

ABOVE A giant halibut, weighing 357 pounds, caught in October 1947

smart society dining tables. Their cousin, the lemon sole, has smoother skin and is best caught after dark.

The remarkable thing about young flatfish is that they come into the world looking like normal-shaped fish, but as they grow their left eye starts to move around their head until it has taken up position forward of the right eye. When this happens the fish starts to lie on its left side, so that both eyes are uppermost – a difficult childhood by anyone's reckoning.

Ireland & Itchen

IRELAND AND ANGLING. PUT these two words into a search engine and you will get 1.6 million hits. The Irish are fanatical about fishing, and they have every kind, from trout to tuna and from tope to tench.

Ireland's wet western climate means it comprises many rivers and loughs of various sizes, making up over 7,000 miles of riverbank and 3,000 miles of coastline. Lightly fished and often free of charge, the Emerald Isle has a natural west/east divide, with coarse fishing practised more in the mid and east, and game fishing in the west. The great limestone loughs of Mask and Corrib used to be held up as fine examples of mixed fisheries, with huge trout and some of the biggest pike in Europe happily co-existing. However, a conflict of interest developed, and game fishing concerns netted and removed many

RIGHT Prolific sport with fish like these bream have made Ireland popular with anglers

pike to preserve stocks of wild brown trout, which caused pike anglers great consternation.

Trout fishing is advertised on many roadside signs, and the local pub is one of the best places to pick up a ticket and find out the best local tactics, along with a pint of Guinness.

The colour of the trout can mirror the colour of the water, the dark-spotted trout of Lough Mask contrasting with the silvery trout of nearby Lough Carra. A Green Peter fly, which imitates the nymphal stage of the mayfly, is a fine pattern to use in May and June. The limestone rocks support bountiful insect life, and this culminates in the mayfly hatch, when dapping is a traditional occupation.

Bream are one of the most common coarse fish species found in Ireland, with large catches possible from its system of rivers, loughs and canals, and fish of up to 10 lb are taken. Tench, rudd, roach and hard-fighting hybrids abound, as do the pike that feed on them. Ireland is famed for its big pike, with several fish of over 50 lb having been caught or found dead in the past two centuries, and English pike anglers who make an annual pilgrimage there

ABOVE Ireland has over 7,000 miles of river bank and attractive waters like Lough Erne

believe the vast waters have the potential still to turn up a surprise.

Fred Buller's famous volume The Domesday Book of Mammoth Pike maintains that the biggest pike ever recorded come from Ireland's River Shannon, a fish of 92 lb found around 1815, closely followed by two of 90 lb, in 1862 and in 1926.

Over 80 species of sea fish can be caught around Ireland's coast, as it sits between cool north Atlantic waters and the warming influence of the North Atlantic Drift, or Gulf Stream. This can bring some unusual warm-water species such as trigger fish, red mullet, red bream, sunfish and amberjack.

Off the rocky shores, sea anglers fish

for bass, pollack and wrasse, while one of the great experiences of Irish sea angling is to fish a west coast storm beach when a big surf is running in the Atlantic: tope can be caught along the coast of Clare, Galway and Mayo.

Itchen

ITCHEN RIVER WATER IS SO CLEAR that you can see even the tiny water boatmen darting past a trout's lifting gills as it hangs motionless between the flowing fronds of aquatic weed. Nylon leaders need to be fine, anglers' clothes

BELOW Ireland is famed for its pike fishing sport

bespoke, and the mown grass banks well tended. Chalkstream fishing is quintessentially English, with traditions steeped in history and protocol closely observed.

The River Itchen rises near Winchester, in Hampshire, and flows into the sea at Southampton, every inch a classic chalkstream. The River Test, its sister river, runs parallel due west of it. Both run over chalk and limestone, and have a languid speed of flow which allows light to penetrate and nurture nutrient-rich vegetation that in turn attracts the insects needed to support great fish populations.

In among the waving aquatic vegetation lie some of the UK's largest wild brown trout, and in winter grayling can be caught on fly in the Itchen, while the lower reaches of the Test attract a run of spring salmon.

But not all of the trout in these chalkstreams are as pure and wild as one might imagine. Around 25 years ago a strain of small but perfectly formed fish from Loch Leven were introduced to boost the natural stock once sought by such angling luminaries as Messrs Halford, Skues, Sawyer and Grey. And many of the offspring of these perfect trout have since been

used to stock waters in Africa, Latin America and Kashmir.

However, the stocking of chalk-streams with lesser quality fish to satisfy increasing commercial demands has led to the cross-breeding of some stockies with the wild brownies, something the Environment Agency is trying hard to control.

An Itchen trout will feed at specific points, usually under the thickest over-hanging branch, or will patrol a distinct zone with regularity. Dry flies such as a Blue-winged Olive, a Pale Evening Dun or a Greenwell's Glory have to be cast to land just upstream of the rising fish, so that it floats down over its nose looking for all the world like an innocent and juicy insect.

Observing the natural insect life above and below the water is part of the skill, since correct form and size of the fly is the most important factor in out-witting an elusive fish. And even if you have selected correctly a large spent mayfly with wings akimbo or a tight-winged cinna-mon sedge, you will still need to cast it with great precision, or that may be the only chance at that fish that you will get.

June & Jump

JUNE IS THE MONTH OF GREAT expectations, when the three-month wait for the end of the traditional Close Season comes to an end at midnight, heralding the Glorious 16th. In recent times this annual respite has been lifted on stillwaters and canals, but many anglers still hang up their rods on March 15 out of respect for their quarry and its breeding season.

But come June 16, the lure of a new season draws them back, with images of bright-topped floats cast into gaps between lily pads and fat tench lured into a false sense of security by the long, angler-free lay-off.

Chris Yates caught his then record carp of 51 lb 8 oz on June 16 during a trip to Redmire Pool, having dreamed he would do just that – the perfect fish at the perfect time.

But contrary to the image, June on

the rivers is usually a disappointment. They will be better in late September and early October, when fish feel the onset of winter and feed hard on autumn's harvest to see them through until the spring.

Jack pike will be lively and 'lairy' in June, bristling with territorial indignation and easy to provoke into chasing a plug or spinner. Their tailwalking antics in summer make up for what they lack in size, and great sport can be had on light tackle by the roving angler armed with a box of lures and a spinning rod.

Bream, too, love the warmth of June, being one of the first to sulk when the weather turns cold. Given half a chance

CENTRE A cold spring can lead to heavyweight tench on June 16.

whole of the pond, moving snake-like over the bottom scavenging their share of nature's casualties.

The trout angler has reservoirs that dimple with the rings of rising trout in June as the light fades, and hungry brownies and rainbows feast on buzzers and sedges caught in the surface film as they struggle to hatch in the calm.

And for the sea angler there are summer species such as black bream and mackerel to catch and bass and pollack to spin for on the long languid evenings, while flounder will be enjoying worms and peeler crabs in the muddy estuaries.

BELOW A bright-topped float cast into a gap between lily pads is the image of the start of the coarse season.

they will bask in shallow water lit by sunshine and feed over a bed of bait in deeper water at dusk.

Rudd kiss the surface of lakes in June, sipping down insects and longing to find a stray piece of bread missed by the ducks as they squabbled for their free feed.

Big carp bask on the surface or shelter under the branches of overhanging trees, rashly believing they are safe from the attentions of anglers and threatening to drop their guard.

And warm summer nights are made for eel fishing if the moon is hidden from view. Then they creep out of their holes in the mud and patrol the

ABOVE Are parasites the cause of coarse fish jumping?

Jump

JUMPING FISH ARE, TO MISQUOTE Churchill, a riddle wrapped in a mystery inside an enigma. Why fish jump has been a subject for speculation since the first time an angler saw a fish leave its natural element, at considerable cost in energy, and return a fraction of a second later with a splash.

Some have made a study of jump patterns, to find out if there is a language that can be interpreted. Trout that rocket through the surface film of a reservoir several feet into the air, emerging vertically like a Polaris missile, are thought to have risen at speed from depth to grab a fly and are merely overshooting their target. The more sedate head-and-tail rises of browsing fish indicate sub-surface feeding.

Carp are said to jump to rid themselves of parasites or to clear silt from their gills, but sometimes hooking a fish will cause others to splash in sympathy on the surface. Carp anglers stay away at night to listen for fish 'crashing', to indicate where on the lake they are feeding. If a carp jumps out in the day-time, it is uncanny how often a bait cast to that

Mackerel can be caught on almost any flashy object when they venture close in on high tides, whipping the surface to spray while chasing sprats and whitebait along the coast.

Thornback ray will be on their summer sand bank feeding haunts before moving into deeper water in October, and may be tempted by a whole sprat on a size 2/0 hook.

Roll on summer, and roll on June 16 – a date to quicken the pulse of every true angler.

spot will result in a run soon after.

But don't be confused by spawning fish. Any carp repeatedly splashing in weedy margins or against islands in warm weather is likely to have far more urgent matters on its mind than inspecting your bait to see if it is worthy of attention.

The most readily understandable jump is the one employed by a hooked fish in a bid for freedom, either by breaking the line or shaking the hook. Some species are more inclined to jump than others. Hook a rainbow trout and it is odds on that it will take to the air several times while being played, but hook a brown trout and there will be repeated attempts to reach the lake bottom.

Garfish are related to flying fish, and will spend most of the time in the air when hooked, perhaps assuming that their adversary must be in the water. While a fish is beneath the surface, its full weight is supported, but once it takes to the air its weight can apply direct pressure on the line, with disastrous results. There is some debate as to

LEFT Hook a rainbow trout and it is odds on that it will take to the air several times

whether the rod tip should be dropped so as not to pull the hook, or whether the line must be kept tight to maintain pressure on the fish.

Pike like to jump when hooked, and bream at Old Bury Hill lake, in Surrey, have a remarkable tendency to take to the air in a way that is quite uncharacteristic for that species. Even fry jump when pursued by predators, skittering across the surface in a silvery shower when a perch or trout strikes.

Whitebait harried by a shoal of mackerel or bass will hurl themselves on to the stones of a beach to escape capture, proving an easy meal for any passing seagull.

And worthy of a special mention are chub, who have the uncanny (or should that be canny?) knack of jumping out of the mouth of a keepnet when the angler who caught them is not looking.

Salmon, also called 'the leaper', are driven by their primeval urge to return to their spawning grounds, and can perform vertical leaps of 12 ft up waterfalls. Mako and thresher sharks may put in a couple of dramatic jumps if hooked by mistake, and part your puny line, and sharks in a feeding frenzy have been known to overshoot the bait and join the angler in the boat.

But the kings of jumping are big game fish such as tarpon, marlin and sailfish. Perhaps it is their size that makes the watcher's eyes bulge, but seeing hundreds of pounds of E-type anger leave the water, tailwalk and crash back in is a sight to behold.

BELOW A tench splashes on the surface at Bury Hill Lake in a bid to avoid the net

Knot & Kipper

KNOTS ARE THE CEMENT THAT holds your tackle set-up together. Without the know-how to tie a good knot, you will be constantly frustrated, and more than likely by the biggest fish you hook.

It is the responsibility of every angler to learn how to tie a neat, strong knot so that you won't have to rely on shop-bought versions. It is frustrating enough to be let down by your own inadequacies without falling victim to other people's as well.

There are more different kinds of knots than most people would credit, but as soon as you go fishing you begin to realise why. Hooks with eyes and hooks with spade-ends need to be attached to line, line needs to be joined to line, loops need to be formed, droppers need to be created, backing, shock leaders, stops knots

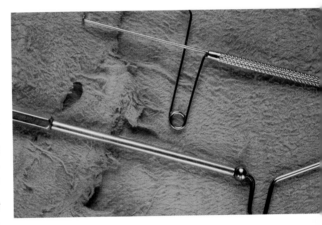

ABOVE Whip finish tools enable fly tyers to finish the pattern with a neat knot at the head

and hairs all need to be attached.

The best thing to do is buy a book of knots and practise them at home, and then ask other anglers to show you what they use. In time you will come to rely on half a dozen different types for different purposes, some customised with

ABOVE Knot pullers allow knots to be tightened fully by improving your grip on the hook

fewer or greater numbers of turns, and remain loyal to these for the rest of your days.

Some anglers favour the old knots, drawn to names like the Bimini Twist, the Palomar, the Blood Bight or the Domhof. The father of modern specimen hunting, Dick Walker, invented the Grinner knot, named after a nickname for his smiling son, using his scientific knowledge to create a knot that did not strangle itself when put under pressure.

Others put their trust in modern creations like the Knotless Knot, which is an ingenious invention that somehow manages to be very strong and reliable despite not seeming to be a knot at all.

But whatever knots you choose, some rules always apply. One is to draw the knot together slowly, reducing friction on the line, which would cause it to heat up and weaken. Another is always to moisten the knot with saliva just before drawing it tight, to cool it and add lubrication. And a third is not to trim the waste end too close to the knot, to allow for it to slip slightly without costing you a fish.

There are knots to join light hook lengths to heavier main lines, knots to join fly lines on to backing, and just as importantly knots to attach the end of your line to your reel. It has been known for a big fish to take all of your line out and test this final knot, and if it fails you will lose fish and line together.

Wind knots are simple overhand loops that can form and tighten on the line during casting. You may not even be aware they are there, or think they are so small that they are insignificant, but a single wind knot can halve the breaking strain of your line. Remove them with a knot-picker if they haven't been pulled too tight, or tackle up again if they are beyond remedy. And renew or re-tie knots that have been pulled hard, either by a large fish or a snag.

Anglers have an armoury of knot tying tools at their disposal, created by ingenious minds as aid to the fumble fingered. Coarse anglers have knot pullers, spade-end hook tyers and loop tyers, while trout anglers have whip finish tools and plastic connectors.

The Turle knot presents the dry fly to its best effect, the tucked Half Blood knot is one of the most popular for attaching a hook or fly, while the Water Knot is mentioned in A Treatyse of Fysshynge wyth an Angle as a way to join horses' hair, and it is still the best knot for tying on droppers.

Braid requires a different set of knots from monofilament, and fluorocarbon works best with different knots from both of them.

Pike anglers use crimps to attach hooks to wire, which is too springy to submit to being tied in a knot. Sea anglers use all of the above knots as well as others for attaching two hooks in a row, to mount larger baits for bigger fish. They are simple to tie and are ideal for hooking up strips of squid or long ragworms.

BELOW Hook tyers make it easier to whip on spade-end hooks

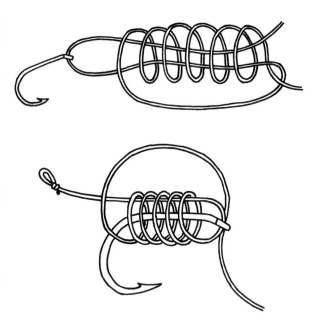

Kipper

KIPPERS ARE A SATURDAY MORNING treat. Heated up with a poached egg on top and slice of brown bread on the side. Mouthwatering to me as I write this, but probably not to everyone reading it.

'Kippering', as I call it, is an example of olde-worlde food preparation involving the curing and smoking of herring or haddock netted in the seas around Britain. The smoking of herring, known as 'silver darlings', is an age-old tradition that is now protected by EC labelling laws in the same way that catching herring has been restricted by European law.

Only the plumpest herring with the correct oil content are used to produce kippers. Technological innovation has long since made redundant the 'herring girls' who historically used to measure, split, gut and wash the fish at a rate of eight per minute. Now, ancient machines that haven't changed since the 1960s do this more than six times faster.

ABOVE Dick Walker's Grinner knot (top) and the popular Knotless Knot

Always remember that no matter how urgent the desire to get fishing or how fleeting the window of opportunity, never rush the tying of a knot. One who hurries the tying of knots is like a person who plays with fire – sooner or later he will get burned, and feel that sickening sensation of a suddenly slack line and the sight of a curly pig-tail of nylon where the hook should have been.

Once the herring have been prepared they are soaked in a brine solution for a length of time dictated by size. This helps to preserve and flavour them, and dates back to when fridges were not available. Importantly, a proper, traditional kipper contains no dye at all.

Then the fish are smoked, which involves tying them together and hanging them on hooks in cavernous smokehouses or special casks. Fires of whitewood shavings and oak sawdust are placed under the rows of herring, which smoulder away for up to 16 hours before they can be called kippers. A couple of hours to cool and then off to market.

Loch Fyne is famous for its kippers, and Manx kippers from the Isle of Man can be obtained by post, as can Craster kippers from the Northumbrian coast, and Arbroath smokies (smoked haddock). Give them a try, for a taste of days gone by.

• For information on obtaining kippers contact: Seafood Industry Authority, 18 Logie Mill, Logie Green Road, Edinburgh EH7 4HG, tel: 0131 558 3331   www.seafish.org

LEFT Anglers can smoke their catch with a purpose-made product

Line & Lake

seed oil, drying in an oven, roughing up with hair brushes and polishing with stone wheels - 16 times for good line and up to 24 times for superior line, a process that took six months from start to finish.

The line had to be dried after use and required periodic oiling, but compared to horsehair it worked miraculously well. Meanwhile, leaders were made from silkworm gut, drawn from the bowels of a silkworm in fine, extremely strong threads for leaders of 4 ft to 9 ft long.

Not surprisingly, fish in those days had to be played and not hoisted in. But the advent of monofilament line revolutionised fishing, though the breaking strains could be a little suspect. Even today, lines are often under strength.

A popular misconception is that, for example, a 4 lb breaking strain line will

LINE MANUFACTURE HAS COME A long way since the days up to the 1800s when braided horsehair or horsehair and silk were the standard materials.

When cotton and flax lines arrived, a manufacturing process was performed which involved soaking in lin-

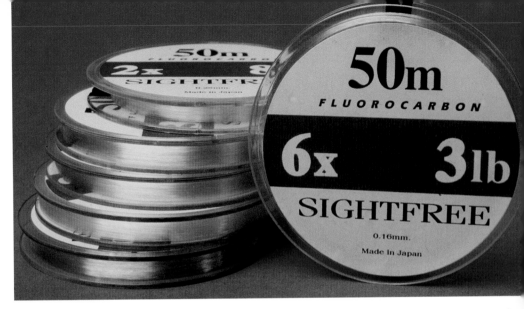

land a 4 lb fish, whatever the circumstance. But a sudden shock, such as an overzealous strike, can exert a much greater force. I confess I've been broken by trout no bigger then 7 oz or 8 oz, due to my overeager response to a sudden take.

Line comes in a mind-boggling array of different colours, breaking strains, diameters, types, makes, lengths and materials. Anglers almost need a science degree to keep up with them. Where once there was simply monofilament, and maybe Dacron for sea anglers, there is now Double Strength line, fluorocarbon, various braids, and a host of proprietary hook length materials from Silkworm to Snake Bite, not to mention shock absorbers such as Powergum.

Monofil comes in clear, green, brown, blue, yellow, black (Amnesia), and braid has just as many choices, along with multicoloured versions dyed different shades along their length for camouflage.

Breaking strains were once measured in pounds, but now you are as likely to hear anglers discussing what millimetre diameter line they were using. And spools that once held 100 yards have swollen in size to take thousands of

ABOVE Fluorocarbon is said to be almost invisible beneath the surface

metres, so that anglers can buy in bulk and save money while spooling up large-capacity reels.

Monofilament is the first choice of most anglers, but braid now has a following among big fish anglers and spinning enthusiasts, in particular because its low stretch means that every knock and bump of the bait is registered on the rod top.

When stalking big fish at close quarters, the elasticity of monofil can be a saving grace, preventing a breakage when the water erupts and the feeding

fish feels the hook and bolts. And the stiffness of some monofilament lines make them preferable for fly fishing, where droppers need to stand clear of the leader, and the cast needs to turn over neatly for perfect presentation.

Beachcasting anglers tie heavier shockleaders, made of lengths of strong nylon, on to the main line to act as a cushion and allow heavy weights to be cast long distances without the main line snapping. Champion casters can reach distances of up to 250 metres with specially built rods and a following

RIGHT Fly lines come in a wide range of colours, sizes and tapers

wind, though often the fish are found closer in, especially in rough weather.

The major drawback to nylon is that it breaks down over time with exposure to light, and so should be purchased 'fresh' several times a season. There have been calls for the boxes it is sold in to be date stamped, but neither the tackle industry nor the retailer would welcome the prospect of goods suddenly being given a shelf life.

Fluorocarbon does not suffer from this problem, and having a refractive index very close to water is said to be truly invisible beneath the surface. Certainly, many anglers swear by its ability to get them bites. However, its price, its knot strength and its abrasion resistance have prevented it from replacing monofilament, and it is used primarily for hook lengths and trout leaders.

Fly lines are polymer based and are graded in a series of sizes, tapers and densities to match the style of fishing. A DT6F is a double-taper number six, floating line, perfect for chasing brownies with a five or six weight rod and tiny dry flies. A WF8S, or weight-forward number eight sinking line, would be better suited to large reservoirs and weighted nymphs or lures. Fly lines are

ABOVE Grasmere in the Lake District is an example of the scenic beauty Britain's lakes have to offer

around 30 metres long and attached to the reel by 100 metres or more of thinner diameter backing.

Before leaving lines and moving to the lakes I must add a word of warning that, left lying around, they can present a danger to wildlife. Take your leftover line home and burn it or cut it into short lengths, whereby it cannot do any damage if lost.

Lake

LAKE FISHING IN BRITAIN CAN involve visiting some of our most beautiful and scenic stillwaters, from the majesty of the Lake District to the simple beauty of the village pond. Such

diversity of attractions is what makes lake fishing so enjoyable – so many waters of such tranquil beauty and all subtly different from the next.

In a sedate pond in Kent, with its overhanging willows brushing the surface, roach fry flash in the shallows, while their larger brethren hang back among the safety of the weed. In a shallow moat in Norfolk, tench nose mosquito larvae from the bottom, sending up streams of pin-head bubbles.

In a gravel pit in Oxfordshire, perch lie in ambush beside bull rushes, even cannibalising their own young, and in a farm pond in Somerset, moorhens cluck at the water's edge, and bream send up clouds of mud, staining the water.

In a Welsh mountain lake or lyn high in the hills, midges dance over the surface watched by hungry wild trout blessed with vivid markings, while a clinker-built boat eases across a glass-surfaced Cumbrian lake surrounded by sleeping giant Fells.

Whether you fish for fresh-run sea-trout in a Scottish loch or visit a newly created fishery designed for anglers and ringed with platforms, the peace that comes from just being beside a motionless pool of water never fades.

Maggot & Minnow

MAGGOTS ARE AN ANGLER'S BEST friend. Easy to obtain, ready to use, and eaten by almost everything that swims, their popularity is such that many anglers won't leave home without them. Even predators like pike, perch and trout can't resist their seductive wriggle, and chub and barbel can be driven into a feeding frenzy by them.

Buying your first pint of maggots in a tackle shop is as much a rite of passage as buying your first pint of beer in a pub. But with them comes a burden of responsibility. You need to prolong their metamorphosis from juvenile grub to adult fly for as long as it takes to use them, so you need to beg permission to put them in the fridge, or at least on the cold garage floor. Remember to close the lid!

With all the fuss of looking after 'livestock', you might have thought the

ABOVE Maggots in various colours and sizes are the first choice bait for many anglers

maggot would be superceded by the more convenient baits, such as pellets and boilies, where cost and waste are kept to a minimum. But the humble maggot still has mass appeal.

Maybe tradition partly explains the continuing appeal of the pint of

In the 1960s and 70s sour-bran specials were fattened on milk, and silky soft gozzers so beloved of bream were bred as a secret weapon by matchmen.

These days maggot farms deliver the goods to tackle shops and other outlets in refrigerated lorries, to slow their development into the static, crisp and

maggots. Our forefathers hung carcasses over the water, and when the eggs laid by bluebottles hatched out, the larvae dropped one by one into the water, attracting hungry fish. A less-time consuming alternative is to hang a bag of bait pierced with holes from an overhanging tree, or to pour a quantity of maggots on to a footbridge and leave them to wriggle over the edge into the water one at a time.

Before maggots entered mass production, anglers 'grew' their own, including a few 'specials' intended only for the hook. In 1790, The Art of Angling suggested that dead flesh, beast's liver or suet were good for maggot production, and if they were needed in early spring, a dead cat or kite buried in the ground over winter was said to produce the goods.

crunchy pre-adult pupal stage also beloved of fish, known as the caster.

In a few areas maggots are sold in vending machines on petrol station forecourts, but you can't beat freshly bred bait from a shop that handles hundreds of pints a week.

Shop-bought maggots come in a

variety of colours and three main types, according to the species of fly that created them. Bronze, red and white are the most popular colours, and you can choose from standard maggots (bluebottles), pinkies (greenbottles) and squatts (houseflies). All have their uses, depending on the size of your quarry and the fickleness of its feeding mood.

Pinkies are slightly smaller than standard maggots and unusual in that their bodies have tiny hairs, which enable them to climb out of the vertical sides of an open bait box. Be warned! Squatts are smaller still, and work well added to groundbait, in particular for bream, which will grub around on the lake or river bed for hours looking for them.

Store your maggots in a container with holes, to allow them to breathe, and keep them in a little sawdust, maize meal or bran, to allow them to clean themselves of any traces of the rotting material on which they were raised.

You might think that the attraction of maggots depends on their wriggliness, but dead maggots are accepted readily by fish, and have the bonus of not squirming away into the lake mud. Maggots can be killed by scalding them with hot water or by

LEFT Maggot farms keep the country's tackle shops supplied with bait

ABOVE Many a young angler's first fish was a minnow

freezing them in bags, and then they will lie on the bottom until found by a shoal of fish.

Maggots placed in a bait box of water will take the liquid on board, turning from a sinking bait into a floating one, opening up all sorts of possibilities. They can be fished on the surface or anchored just off the bottom or used to counterbalance the weight of a hook for more natural presentation. But remember to keep an eye on them - wet maggots can climb vertical surfaces and go anywhere and everywhere, and probably will.

Some anglers flavour their maggots with fruity essences, sweet powders or spices such as turmeric, saying it disguises the human scent the bait can pick up on being handled. Others fish them three at a time in different colours, recreating the strip of their favourite football team.

Minnow

MINNOWS ARE THE THE FISHES' environmental inspector for water quality in that they are the first species to react to pollution and will either quit the waterway or roll over and die if the pollution is severe. They also provide important food for larger species, as well as many a young angler's first fishy encounter, satisfying an urge to fish that can remain with us for the rest of our lives.

To catch minnows for bait, forget hooks and line. A plastic bottle cut off at the top and stapled inside the base of a second bottle creates a minnow trap. Place some bread and stones inside and lower it into the river.

Perch and trout are particularly fond of minnows, as shown by the naming of flies such as the deer hair Muddler Minnow, and spinners like the traditional Devon Minnow, which has a sleek, tubular metal body, painted eyes and a pair of propeller-like fins at the front. Watching the speed of real minnows in a current can teach us alot about the speed at which our lures should be fished and the reason that many fish take as the lure hits the water, is because that's the only time it's travelling at the right speed.

The term 'minnow' has taken on a derogatory meaning, being used to describe any organisation or football team of diminutive status. But these underdogs have the power to produce a shock. If you are ever up-country in the States and feel a tap on your line, you may find yourself face to face with the largest native American minnow, the endangered Colorado pikeminnow. At up to six feet in length and 80 lb in weight, this isn't a minnow to be messed with.

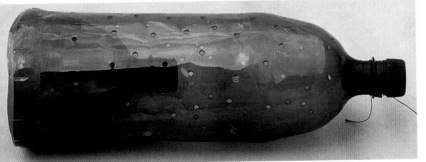

LEFT A minnow trap can be made from two old plastic bottles

Net & Night

NETS ARE OFTEN A SOURCE OF great consternation among anglers, but are an essential item of equipment. Manufacturers argue over whose nets are kindest to fish, fishery owners introduce keepnet bans, and wives and mothers complain about the smelly puddles of water they leave behind after every outing.

Landing nets and keepnets are the most forgotten items of fishing tackle when setting out for a day's sport, presumably because they don't figure in our plans until we have hooked a fish, and by then it's too late.

Most commercial stillwaters insist nets are dipped in a vat of anti-bacterial solution at the entrance to the fishery, to prevent the spread of disease from one lake to another. And many waters decree that match anglers use two keepnets - one to retain the carp they catch until

CENTRE The design of keepnets is constantly evolving

the weigh-in, and one for the smaller species, to protect these from damage by their bulky brethren.

But for all the inconvenience, there is nothing quite like driving home from a successful outing with the odour of a well-used net wafting from the back of the car, reminding you of the sport you have just enjoyed.

A Chinese drawing dating from 1195 shows a form of keepnet made from cane ribs, and The Art of Angling (1577) acknowledges the use of nets to retain catches. These days nets are made from super-soft, fine-weave mesh that dries quickly and is kind to fish, provid-

sales of antique tackle.

Specimen hunters have developed their own retention aids, namely sacks and tubes. Sacks are soft, synthetic, fine-mesh bags with a drawstring or zip at one end, in which big fish can be kept overnight in deeper water than the margins, for a photo call the next morning. Tubes are like small keepnets made from sack-type material that can be staked out in rivers, with fish like barbel and pike facing into the flow while they recover their strength.

BELOW Tubes are like small keepnets made from sack-type material

ing them with a dark tunnel in which to shelter until the session is over.

Modern landing nets often comprise two types of mesh - a fine one in the base, to protect the fish, and a wider one at the sides, to make them easier to manoeuvre in fast-moving water. Ghost landing nets, made from light-coloured nylon, became popular for a while because they are said to be less visible to fish as they are about to be landed, but questions were asked concerning their abrasive qualities.

Knotted nets were outlawed in the 1970s for this reason, and only now show themselves in old photos and at

rolling around on the bottom.

Conservation is the name of the game, with anglers staking out nets with a bankstick through the loop in the base, or seeking somewhere shady to put them. In some matches there is a half-time weigh-in and the fish are returned, to cause them as little stress as possible, and many pleasure anglers do without keepnets completely.

But certain species are said to be easier to catch if not returned. Perch in particular are rumoured to take the rest of the shoal away if the caught ones are returned, and to make a big catch of bream it is said that the caught fish should be retained, to avoid disturbing the rest of the shoal.

Landing nets come in all shapes and sizes, from round and oval to triangular and spoon-shaped. Their frames can be carbon fibre, metal, plastic or one side of cord, and vary in depth from 'pan' (like a frying pan) to generously deep for pike and carp. Mobile anglers like to sling their nets over their back or hang them from their waistband.

Sea anglers use drop-nets on long cords when a high pier prevents landing by any other means, but handling one in rough weather is an art in itself.

Keepnet design is constantly evolving, with zips and flaps being built-in to allow access to the fish more easily when weighing the catch, and with square 'rings' instead of round, to stop the net

Big sea and game fish were once routinely gaffed, using a steel hook on a pole, or in the case of salmon, tailed, whereby a loop of strong material 'lassoed' the tail. These days, nets are much more common, especially with catch and release now prevalent on salmon rivers, or fish are beached, to be unhooked in the margins.

But many an angler who has eschewed the use of a net has been left cursing his laziness when the hook pulled at the last second. The risk of losing a fish by swinging it in or picking it up is not worth it, except maybe the odd mackerel from a line of five dangling from your feathers.

And never let a stranger net your fish. Success with the net is all about timing and gauging when the fish is ready. An inexperienced or overenthusiastic person who grabs the net will lunge at the fish when he sees it, eager to play his part in its capture but unwittingly encouraging its escape as it flees the implement.

Wait until a fish is ready, having taken a gulp of air, and showing a willingness to lie on its side, and then draw it over the net with the rod without chasing the fish with the net.

Night

NIGHT FISHING CAN GIVE AN angler a piscatorial adrenaline rush of the highest level, but also scare him witless. I was once fishing an estuary pool for sea-trout in Scotland (the only beat I can afford) in the pitch black, when suddenly I heard a roaring noise downstream. It seemed to be getting louder

BELOW Night fishing can be an intoxicating and addictive side of the sport.

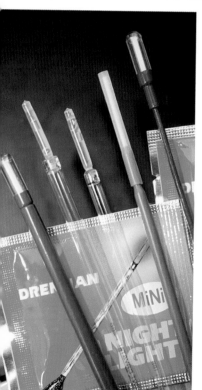

BELOW Float anglers fit glowing Starlites or Betalights to their float tips

and louder, and though I strained my eyes I couldn't see anything. With the clattering of stones I imagined a huge tidal wave of water rushing towards me. Then the moon came out and I could half see a herd of deer moving away fast over the outline of a dark hill.

Most coarse and sea fish feed at dawn and dusk, and many continue on into the dark, providing the angler with the best chance of hooking something big and wary. It can also be the most testing and dangerous form of fishing, though it may not seem so when you are tucked up in bed in a warm bivvy tent, a pack of beer at your elbow and a stove beside you, and a pair of slippers at the ready.

But wading a pool for sea-trout on a moonless night is a different matter, and the key to success and survival is knowing the water. Go there in daylight and find out the depth, or if you are fishing from the bank arrive in daylight, and have everything ready to-hand.

Float anglers fit glowing Starlites or Betalights to their float tips to see them in the gloom, while carp anglers use electronic bite alarms that double as rod rests and light up and bleep when they get a run.

Match anglers also get in on the action, as several commercial stillwaters now have floodlights erected around their lakes for special contests held after dark.

Despite the inconvenience, fishing at night can be well worth the trouble because sometimes crafty fish become nocturnal feeders, only taking baits after dark to avoid capture. They venture close in when darkness falls, keen to make up for lost feeding time, and that's when you can be there waiting for them.

Night fishing can be an intoxicating and addictive side of the sport, full of heightened senses and heartstopping moments. Everyone should try it once, just to see if it's for you.

Otolith, Ouse & Otter

OTOLITHS ARE THE 'EARBONES' within the inner ears of fish, and consist of white, chalk-like secretions built up over the life of the fish. They also provide fish with a sense of balance, in much the same way as our inner ear does for us. All fish have them, with the exception of sharks, rays and lampreys.

You may be thinking that fish don't have ears, or at least not visible ones, and there is some debate as to whether they can hear. They may rely solely on sensory receptors located elsewhere on their bodies, such as along the lateral line - a line running along the middle of the flank from head to tail.

Another value of the otolith is in determining the age of a fish. The white chalky material is laid down year by year, and can be read in a similar way to the growth rings in a cross-section of a tree.

With modern technology a fish's life history can be reconstructed - from its year of birth and its migration pathways to the temperature of the water in which it swam - providing invaluable information for biologists and fishery scientists.

Whether fish can 'hear' may be up for debate, but what isn't in question is that they are sensitive to the slightest vibration through the water. Stumble on the bank and every fish in the vicinity will head for the hills. Some fish have better hearing than others. Marlin are said to have otoliths no bigger than a pinhead, whereas those of other fish are the size of a penny.

A few anglers even go so far as to whisper when talking close to the water. I go along with their cautious approach if addressed by a whisperer, and reply in similar, hushed tones out of politeness.

The time to worry is when the angler says his motive for whispering is not to reduce sound vibrations but because the fish might hear what he was saying.

Ouse

OUSE IS A WORD THAT IS DEAR TO many anglers' hearts today. The Yorkshire Ouse is popular with both matchmen and specimen hunters, containing as it does most coarse fish species, some to an impressive size. But it is the Great Ouse, in particular where it runs through Bedfordshire and Buckinghamshire, that quickens the pulse of some of the country's top anglers.

Fish growth rates on the Great Ouse have been phenomenal in recent years, with huge barbel, perch and chub causing anglers to re-evaluate what is and isn't a big specimen.

Where once a 14 lb barbel was the fish of the season nationwide, now it barely rates a mention, and the British record has been beaten again and again by Great Ouse fish until it is close to 20 lb.

Perch anglers who considered the catching of a 4 lb fish to be a major achievement now find themselves catching more than one in a session on the Ouse. And 6 lb chub are caught regularly, so it is 7 lb fish that merit a mention in the news.

A narrow stretch of streamy water at Adams Mill has become a Mecca for barbel anglers, having produced a string of records, and there is a waiting list for a syndicate season ticket to fish that hallowed ground.

Numerous theories abound as to the reason for this galloping growth rate, from a plentiful supply of anglers' high-protein bait to the spread of foreign crayfish throughout the river. But some argue that the current years of plenty will be followed by years of lack, because the small fish that will guarantee future sport are not present.

BELOW Ouse perch like this brace are drawing anglers from far and wide

Otter

OTTERS WERE ONCE PERCEIVED TO be the angler's enemy, and were to be hunted with otter hounds and driven from many riverside habitats. But thankfully that is now history, and the otter is enjoying a revival throughout Britain's waterways.

Today's angler enjoys watching wildlife, and gets close to a wide variety of different species simply by sitting quietly for long periods waiting for a bite. The image of a robin perching on a rod and fluttering down to steal a maggot from the angler's bait box is a fairly common occurrence.

Few anglers now begrudge otters their catch. I recall a wonderful night of catching sea-trout in Scotland and having to protect my catch from the attentions of a particularly inquisitive sea otter. At least otters are tidy hunters and will usually eat the whole of any fish they catch.

But mink kill for pleasure, and even when not hungry. If not trapped and culled they will destroy fish stocks and wildlife and displace the native otter.

BELOW Otters are enjoying a revival, and few anglers would begrudge them their fish

OPPOSITE The damage cormorants do to fisheries has led to them being dubbed the 'black death'

Cormorants, herons, red-breasted mergansers and goosanders all take fish, but cormorants are particularly voracious and prolific. The Government issues permits for the control of cormorants, but numbers are in single figures per fishery, while populations run into hundreds on single big reservoirs. No one who has seen a 2 lb trout slip down the throat of a cormorant in a second can doubt the damage that these birds do to fisheries, both coarse and game. No wonder they have been dubbed the 'black death'.

Some argue that predators cannot be blamed for plundering a constantly restocked pantry. I once watched a family of red breasted mergansers, sweep down a chalk stream full of panicking trout. Sometimes the angler can only put down the rod, sit back and just watch and marvel at the efficiency of some of nature's own fish predators.

ABOVE The heron provides fair competition to the angler

Pike & Paternoster

ABOVE Pike have evolved over millions of years into the ultimate predator

PIKE ARE ONE OF BRITAIN'S OLDEST species of fish, having evolved over millions of years into the ultimate killing machine. Everything about them, from their lean, dart-like shape, their sleek, strong jaws and big tail has evolved to propel them at great speed over short distances to snatch their prey. And when those merciless jaws clamp on a roach or bream, the rows of 300 backward-facing teeth are a one-way ticket to oblivion.

LEFT There is hardly a natural water in Britain that does not hold pike of some size

Receptors along the body of pike pick up the tiniest vibrations of potential prey, while their dappled, olive markings provide superb camouflage against the reeds and weed of their home. And their delicate fins allow them to hold station while remaining almost motionless, all but invisible in their watery world.

Fossilised remains of an ancient relative show that pike have remained remarkably similar for thousands of years - a combination of getting it right first time, and "if it ain't broke, don't fix it".

Rivers, lakes, lochs, gravel pits and even canals all hold pike. Indeed, it is claimed that they will spread to any water where they are not present and take their place in the food chain, their eggs said to be carried on the feet of waterbirds. Some anglers dislike them, and prefer waters not to have them because they eat other fish. But in truth it is the sick and dying inhabitants that pike pick off, preferring an easy meal to a difficult one, which is nature's way of maintaining a healthy fish population.

Pike use a combination of sensors, sight and smell to detect their prey, but blind pike are still encountered and caught by anglers, suggesting they do not need all three senses. Fish baits and spinners form the traditional approach for them, through plenty have been caught on flies, or by mistake on worms and maggots.

Mackerel, sardines, herrings, smelt, trout and lamprey eels are the most popular baits, along with coarse fish like small roach and bream, used dead or alive. However, livebaiting is outlawed on some waters, to protect fish stocks and avoid the spread of disease.

Artificial plugs and spinners are designed to look and behave just like a sick or injured fish, wobbling through the water or across the surface as the angler retrieves them. A vast array is available, in particular from America and Scandinavia, and on their day they can prove deadly.

Pike like to lie in wait and ambush their prey, as I discovered one day in Ireland. As I reeled in a plug there was an almighty splash not three metres from the bank, and a swirl that announced the presence of a pike. I cast again, heart pounding and hairs standing on end, and wound in slowly. The pike waited for the plug to pass again, struck, and my rod tip was yanked into the water. Being somewhat inexperienced, I lost the tug of war, and the pike departed with the plug, but it bobbed to the surface a few moments later.

Whether you are float fishing or legering fish baits for pike, or spinning, a wire trace is essential, as a pike's teeth will bite through nylon in a second. And learn how to handle pike with care as for such a professional killer they are a surprisingly fragile fish, and one that presents no danger on the bank to anglers who know what they are doing.

Paternoster

PATERNOSTER MEANS 'OUR FATHER' in Latin, and some would have you believe that the name refers to St Peter's use of a line of hooks with a weight at the bottom to catch fish. He is also said to have left his thumb print on the sides of John Dory (a sea fish).

But more likely is the explanation that paternoster rigs have three-way 'junction points' along their length to which hooks and traces are tied, and a string of rosary beads also has markers at intervals, each one indicating the necessity of saying an Our Father.

Paternoster rigs have been used widely in the Middle Eastern and Mediterranean regions for centuries, and are still used by sea anglers today, with up to three or four hooks sprouting from the main line, depending on the species being pursued. Different baits can be used on each hook, allowing the angler to discover what bait is preferred, and whether any other species are present.

Fish may not be the cleverest of creatures, but they possess a keen sense of danger, and know for sure when a bait is

not behaving as it should. Bass realise that a sandeel should weigh almost nothing in their mouth, and so reject any bait that feels unnatural. But a live sandeel presented on a running paternoster rig allows a big bass to take the bait into its mouth and move away with it without feeling any resistance.

ABOVE Feathering for mackerel involves using a paternoster rig

OPPOSITE Find pike in a feeding mood and several can be caught in quick succession

ter rigs with or without floats and with any number of hooks, in particular when feathering for mackerel, are used, as is one called Count de Moira's Beam.

The basic idea is to suspend the bait at differing levels from the bottom as well as present it as naturally as possible. The Count de Moira's Beam paternoster features, from bottom upwards, a weight attached by 2 ft of nylon to one end of a thin, rigid wire beam, with a fish deadbait on hooks and line suspended from the other end of the beam. From the middle of the beam is tied a length of nylon with a cork, which keeps the beam supported underwater, and up at the surface sits a float, which acts as a strike indicator.

The whole arrangement is quite a contraption, but it involves a lot of fun in the preparation, in a similar vein to the tying of flies. And it does work, and produces the goods. No need for the Angler's Prayer ("Oh Lord, send me a fish so big that even I have no need to lie about its size") when you have a paternoster to catch fish for you.

Paternoster rigs can be adapted for many different uses and for species ranging from bass and bream to pike and perch. Running and fixed paternos-

Quick, Quivertip & Quiet

QUICK IS WHAT THE NON-ANGLING public would expect you to be when performing an act with a name like 'strike'. However, speed is not always what is called for when the strike is applied, as many anglers have found to their cost. The word 'strike' is a slight misnomer, as the action in question is more like a tightening of the line by an upward movement of the rod to connect with the fish that has taken your bait.

However, while many fish require the angler to be on his or her mettle and as quick on the draw as a Wild West gunslinger to connect on the strike, others must be given time to take a bait properly. In some cases size is the determining factor, with the quickest of strikes

being required when walking up a small tumbling stream flicking a fly into tiny pools for juvenile trout. You will also need to be quick when your float dips

BELOW Not all species require the angler to be quick on the draw

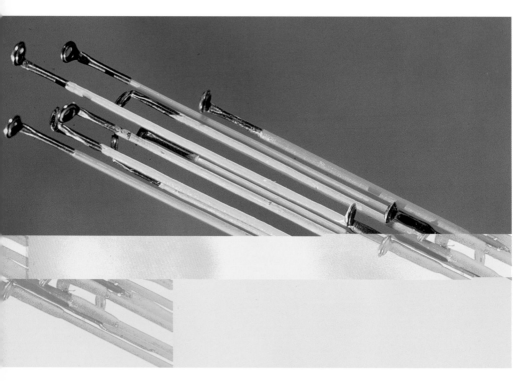

ABOVE Quivertips are ultra-slim tips for coarse fishing rods

under as you trot a stream for dace - one of the fastest biting fish that swims. Often your maggot will come back sucked to a skin by the fish, having been to the back of their throat and out again in an instant.

But other small fish will swallow your bait and wait patiently for you to realise. Small perch don't let the presence of something like a hook spoil their voracious appetite.

The difference lies more in species.

Pike must be allowed time to let them take a bait properly, but don't delay more than a few seconds. A hungry pike may bolt a bait, and removing hooks once they have been swallowed is a harder task than when they are lodged in the mouth, as you get with an earlier strike.

Salmon have their own rules when it comes to striking, and successfully hooking one is an exercise in self-control rather than speed of reaction. The trick is to give line when you feel that first tug and wait, and wait, until you are sure the fish must have taken the fly properly in its mouth and turned away. Only then can you tighten up and lift into the fish to set the hook.

Hardest of all is to fish for trout on a loch or lough that is also home to salmon. When a trout takes your fly you must pause and then strike, and it is heartbreaking to see a salmon take your fly and realise just a split second too late that you should have delayed your strike for longer, while watching your fly plucked from the lips of your prize.

On these occasions it is quickness of mind rather than quickness of reactions that sort the successful anglers from the ones with lots of stories but empty bags at the end of the day.

Quivertip

QUIVERTIPS ARE BITE DETECTORS built into the end of your rod to tell you when to strike when you are legering, which involves fishing a bait held on the lake or river bottom with a weight. It is rather like watching the top of your rod for movement, but with an ultra-slim tip section.

The quivertip has a couple of cousins, the swingtip and the springtip, which screw into the end of your rod and do a similar job but in different conditions and with a different degree of sensitivity.

ABOVE The springtip is a close cousin of the quivertip

There are all manner of devices to allow you to spot bites when you have no float to watch. When a longer wait between bites is involved there are electronic bite alarms with lights and speakers to tell you when a fish is showing some interest, and even wake you from your slumbers.

BELOW Electronic bite alarms tell you when a fish is showing some interest

One of the most successful ways of detecting bites is touch legering. After casting out your lead and bait, just loop the line between the reel and first ring over the forefinger of your rod hand. The sensitivity of your skin will tell you when the line has moved even a fraction. If you are holding the rod at the time, you will find you have struck even before your brain has had time to register that you have had a bite.

Quiet

QUIET IS ONE OF THE GREAT attractions of angling. It offers the chance to escape from the noise pollution of modern life, where there is always an engine being revved, a door being slammed, a dog barking or a baby crying. Sometimes anglers just like to stand and listen to the silence.

Troubles seem to ebb away in silence. Unpaid bills, problems at work or fears for the future seem less pronounced beside the water. Thousands of anglers go fishing at weekends not just to catch fish, but to sit somewhere quiet without interruptions or distractions and allow their thoughts to unravel. Perhaps it is overstating the case to claim that angling is therapy for life, and the saviour of more than a few people's sanity, to say nothing of their marriages, but the counselling affect of angling should not be underestimated.

At its best, angling can be both deeply relaxing and heart-stoppingly exciting. More than a few celebrities spend the few spare moments in their busy lives going fishing because it is the perfect antidote to a hectic life

LEFT Horton Church
Lake, in Berkshire, is in
the flight path for
Heathrow Airport

lived in the spotlight of constant public and media attention.

The exception is when the lure of
big fish causes you to stray into a less
than tranquil place, in the belief that
success will more than compensate for
the lack of tranquility. Gravel work-
ings that are still being operated, lakes
dug alongside main roads and train
lines, and canals fringed by back gar-
dens full of hedgetrimming, lawn-

mowing DIY fanatics spring to mind.

In the heyday of Horton Church
Lake, in Berkshire, anglers put up with
the fact that it was close to the end of
the runway at Heathrow Airport in
order to fish for the finest collection of
big carp in the country. But is the ultimate prize a memorable capture or an
overwhelming feeling of contentment,
for what is success when its price is
peace of mind?

Rod & Reel

RODS HAVE BEEN USED TO CATCH
fish since ancient Egyptians first waved
them around in 2000 BC. But it took
another 4,000 years before the rod as we
know it today came about, with line

running through its rings rather than
being fixed to the end.

The idea of having rings led to the
invention of the reel, allowing bigger
fish to be caught by the art of playing
them into submission.

Natural fibrous materials were the
first choice for making rods, and reed
was the preferred material for many
years. Spanish reed rods were still in use

they were put together with lengths of bamboo when I broke mine in the car door. Machines soon replaced hand-constructed rods, and the first built-cane rods appeared, then ones made from steel alloy tubes. These gave way to solid glass, which in turn led to fibre-glass and then carbon fibre (a byproduct of the aircraft manufacturing industry) and boron. With every technical innovation came an improvement in lightness, strength and rigidity, until today's anglers are spoiled with rods so light, stiff and responsive that our forefathers would have swooned had they held such a tool.

In use, a rod is basically a spring that is loaded and unloaded to propel a bait out across the water to the waiting fish. But what must also be borne in mind is the size of the fish you intend to catch, the distance you wish to fish at and the method you intend to employ, as all will have an important bearing on your choice of rod.

The action of a rod is something that gives many anglers a great deal of pleasure in assessing. If you wander down Fisherman's Row at the CLA Game Fair, in July, you will see hundreds of anglers trying out various rod actions by

until recently, and are the forerunners of today's poles. Greenheart is a hardwood from Guyana, and it was the basis of rod making for many years, despite its weight. An angler needed strong arms and more than a little stamina to wield one all day, and fly anglers certainly kept false casting to a minimum.

The advent of split cane changed my life, until I inadvertently discovered how

CENTRE Old rods and reels were made from heavier materials than today's

whipping them in the air. The action is the feel that the rod has when casting a line and controlling your end tackle, and when bending into a fish.

The finest rods are expensive, but they are as nothing compared to the very best poles, which can set you back several thousand pounds. Poles are basically long rods without rings, the line being attached to the end via a length of elastic to prevent a breakage when a fish is hooked.

Pole fishing is all about speed, and even when sections need to be taken apart to land each fish, this can be done at a rate that will outpace a rod and reel angler.

Not all poles are expensive, though. It is possible to get a perfectly good one for a couple of hundred pounds, and this will allow you pinpoint accuracy of presentation at up to 16 metres out from where you are sitting.

Reels

REELS ARE SAID TO HAVE BEEN invented by the Chinese in 1195, when a device described as a "wheele" appeared in an illustration. In the UK it wasn't until 1651 that the idea of a reel was contemplated, when they were described as a winch bolted on to the

RIGHT Traditionalists still enjoy using centrepin reels for trotting

rod. The idea soon caught on, and various mechanisms came into use in the following years.

The multiplier reel made its first appearance in Rural Sports magazine in 1881, and is still used today for all types of sea fishing, from boat to beachcasting, as well as for salmon spinning in heavy water. Casting with a multiplier reel is something to be practised by the beginner, to prevent the line over-running on the drum. Even with in-built magnetic or centrifugal brakes, a hastily-made cast can lead to an horrendous tangle, known in angling circles as a bird's nest.

The first centrepin reel appeared in 1850, storing line on a free-wheeling drum controlled by subtle pressure on the rim with the angler's thumb. Famous name reels like the Allcock Nottingham and Allcock Aerial still change hands, and some modern versions are made which traditionalists enjoy using for trotting a float or legering for barbel. The lack of a handle on many puts some people off, and the delicate skill of casting by pulling down loops of line is an art in itself, but tackle control and the feeling of direct contact with the bait and fish are second to none.

A big leap forward came in 1884 when a Mr Malloch introduced an all-metal reel that rotated through 90 degrees. This allowed line to spill off the reel as it faced forward, and be retrieved when it was turned back to its original position.

But it was the birth of the fixed-spool reel that captured the angling public's imagination. Easy to use, capable of long casting and with the capacity to hold a lot of line, it was the breakthrough that anglers had been waiting for.

As they were refined, a ratchet anti-reverse was added, and an adjustable clutch to allow fish to take line under a pre-determined pressure. Today's models have free-spool facilities, anti-twist devices and line clips to enable you to cast to the same spot every time, but the design remains largely the same.

The first fly reels were a heavy accompaniment to an already heavy rod, but were great works of art, with wooden inlays and intricate engravings on brass casings. Hardys of Alnwick have always produced reels of great distinction, with suitably aspirational names to match - Princess, Viscount, Perfect, Zenith, and St George. Modern fly reels are cast out of blocks of aerospace aluminium, and boast disc-drag brake systems. Even the new Hardy reel has a handle made from black carbon fibre weave to make it "more comfortable to hold in all types of weather". I fear we have all gone soft.

BELOW Modern day fly reels are light and reliable

Salmon & Spinning

SALMON IS THE KING OF FISHES, prized above all others and angled for by Royalty, but it was not always so. At medieval banquets pike were more highly sought after than salmon, but today the monies paid for the privilege of hopefully doing battle with a salmon reflect its iconic status.

There are those who believe sea-trout make the harder fighter, pound for pound, and that wild salmon have become tainted by farmed fish. But for me Salmo salar is way up there. The symbol of the leaping fish as a metaphor for single-minded determination in adversity and against terrific odds is a potent one, and the story of how it follows its migratory urges to spawn and then descend to the sea perhaps to die is a tragedy of Shakespearean proportions.

The take of a salmon as it rolls over your fly is a heart-stopping moment, as is the moment when your reel starts its first screaming run, and the rod arches over in a dangerous bend. In 1816 the River Thames produced a massive run of salmon, and Izaak Walton, armed with his 20 ft rod, said he felt that while the north produced the fastest and biggest salmon, the taste of the Thames fish was excellent. The industrial revolution and the turning of the Thames into an open sewer meant that the north and west have become the places to find salmon, though attempts are still made to re-introduce them into the cleaned-up Thames.

Salmon begin their life as eggs in the gravel runs in the upper reaches of rivers, and hatch and grow into parr. After around two years they undergo a physiological change that affords them the impressive ability to be able to live in both fresh and sea water, and as smolts they migrate down river to the sea.

Here they travel as far afield as Greenland, feeding prolifically on sandeels and sea invertebrates such as shrimps, which give salmon flesh its hint of pink, until the urge to breed kicks in. Then these grilse of 3 lb to 8 lb return to the rivers of their birth using their sense of smell to find their way.

Once in freshwater again they stop feeding, and rely on their reserves of fat

RIGHT Traditional salmon flies tied with gut eyes

to carry them through the journey up river. Often they have to wait for rain to provide them with enough water to move from one pool to the next and reach the redds to spawn, before dropping back down as kelts.

Salmon fishing is the big brother of trout fishing, employing stouter rods on larger rivers for bigger fish. Traditional salmon flies are impressive beasts with names to match, like Willie Gunn, Garry Dog, Jock Scott, Munro Killer, Black Doctor and General Practitioner. Marrying all of the materials needed to make them according to the pattern takes great skill and patience.

Smaller, modern hair-wing flies such as the Ally's Shrimp, Hairy Mary and Stoat's Tail are much in use today, or at times of high and coloured water anglers may spin or leger worms or prawns when rules allow.

It is a puzzle why salmon take anything in freshwater, when their stomachs are always found to be empty. Theories have been debated over the years as to why this should happen, and it seems that certain temperatures and water conditions can trigger an instinctive reaction that spurs fish to take a bait.

But what is without question is the

salmon's dedication to duty, willing to overcome impossible obstacles, leap waterfalls and stop at nothing to achieve its aim. This is a king among fishes, and a hero worthy of our admiration.

ABOVE Netting a salmon on the Thurso

Spinning

SPINNING IS OFTEN VIEWED AS only worthy of beginners, employing as it does fairly basic skills, and being a good introduction to the hobby of angling. However, in the hands of a skilled practitioner it is a subtle and deadly art capable of yielding surprising results. The choice of spinner alone requires knowledge and experience, since what is on the end of your line will govern the depth at which you fish and how visible your lure is in the given colour of water.

Casting spinners to within inches of reed beds and working them over snags and stones will produce far better results than throwing hopefully into open water, and a subtle change of tactics to a bigger or smaller lure or a deeper diving vane can make all the difference.

The invention of the swivel allowed the spinner to be created, with dead minnows mounted on spinning rigs and trolled along behind boats, or cast out and wound back in fits and starts. Artificial spinners and plugs were modeled on the real thing, and the first spoon is said to have been created after a silver spoon was dropped into the water by a servant, in around 1830, and was grabbed by a jack (juvenile) pike.

Vivid imagination took over, and lures appeared in a variety of hues. The leather eel-tail, the kidney spoon, the Toby spoon, the Mepps spinner and Rapala plugs followed, and many are still around today. Jerk baits are the latest breakthrough, and though not easy to use, they have accounted for some massive pike.

Sea anglers soon realised that many fish in the sea will take anything that glints, based on the fact that it resembles a bait fish such as a sprat or whitebait. Mackerel will sometimes take a bare hook as it flashes past them, and as a boy I wrapped some silver foil around a hook on a swivel and cast off a pier at high tide, feasting on my catches.

Pollock and bass will take plugs, spinners and rubber eels, and provide memorable sport on light tackle. But remember that foolhardy young 'school' bass under 14 inches long have to be returned, and that successful spinning is no soft option. You've gotta work your spinner hard to fool a worthwhile fish.

ABOVE Pike can find spinners hard to ignore

OPPOSITE Spinning with plugs and lures is a skilful side of the sport

Tweed
& Trout

TWEED IS KNOWN AS 'THE QUEEN of Scottish rivers' being as she is 100 miles long. She rises as a tiny stream in Tweedsmuir, and ends as a mighty river in Berwick, across the Border in England. Many bloody battles have been fought over her banks, while trying to set the Border between the two countries.

Tweed's catchment area is approximately 1,900 square miles, and four main rivers feed into the Tweed - the Teviot, the Till, the Whiteadder and the Ettrick - all noted angling rivers in their own right. The Tweed is known for its salmon, but roach, dace, gudgeon, perch and eels are found in good numbers in the lower reaches, and sea-trout to over 10 lb as well as good grayling and brown trout in the upper reaches of the river.

The cost of fishing the Tweed can be off-putting for all but the wealthy, since to fish there in the autumn can cost £4,000 per rod per week on the famous Junction pool. But what you are buying is a taste of history on a river with an ancient pedigree recorded in fishing journals that boast of 10,000 salmon per annum averaging 8 lb to 10 lb, with a smattering of 20-pounders and the chance of an odd 30-pounder.

Nothing in angling can ever be guaranteed, but those who pay the cash do so in the hope of a tussle with a big,

CENTRE The mighty River Tweed can be hard on the arms and the pocket

fresh-run fish, muscled-up to swim the 80 miles to spawn.

The rods used are as long as in Izaak Walton's day, and are needed to cover the vast width of the main river. In many pools anglers in boats are either let down the river by a gillie on the bank, or rowed slowly down a vast pool for over an hour and a half.

Scotland has many serious salmon rivers which can be fished at affordable rates by holidaying anglers. Ireland, too, is a treat for the salmon angler, and both offer waters framed by magnificent scenery. But how much sport you get will depend largely on when you go and how much you are prepared to pay. Tickets can be brought at post offices, hotels, tackle shops, estate offices or the pub. I would always recommend the latter, as this is where all the serious anglers hang out.

Unlike Tweed which is an autumn-run river, the river Dee has a Royal pedigree for spring-run salmon, helped by the buying out of netting rights at the mouth of the river. Not so the North Esk, once described as the most prolific medium-size salmon river in the world, where heavy sea netting and lower-river netting has drastically reduced the numbers of salmon returning to spawn.

Scotland is full of grand rivers, and the Tay was guaranteed its place in

BELOW Long rods are needed to cover the width of the Tweed

history in 1922 when a certain Miss Georgina caught the biggest salmon ever taken on rod and line in Britain. Its 118 miles include famous beats such as Upper and Lower Scone, Redgorton and Catholes.

And when the salmon are stale and disinterested, there are always wild brownies in lochs and streams, or coarse fish of specimen size. The River Spey, home of the Spey cast employed to avoid the large number of trees along both banks, has large pike in the lochs along its length and Loch Lomond is noted for its perch, roach and giant pike.

Trout

TROUT ARE WIDELY DISPERSED throughout the UK's well-oxygenated rivers and lakes, though how they got to some of their more remote watery habitats beats me. Wandering across the hills I came across a tiny lake or stream at the head of numerous water-falls, and never ceased to be amazed when the rings of a rise betrayed the presence of a tiny brown trout.

Anglers in the past caught so many varieties of trout in the UK that they grouped them into ten types, ranging from the land-locked sea-trout found in the limestone lochs of Sutherland, to cannibal ferox trout caught on deep-trolled spinners. All are, in fact, brown trout, only living in different habitats and adapting to prevalent conditions.

One strain of trout found in the shallow, gravelly waters of Lough Leven was even considered to be blue-blooded enough to ·be used to stock the rich chalkstream waters of the Itchen, where it grew to a prodigious size. Though the breeding of brown trout for stocking has enabled many wild fisheries to maintain their stocks, the definition of what is actually a wild fish may well lie with one of those tiny brownies found in the remotest hill lakes and streams.

There are those who would argue that brown trout tend to fight harder than their cousins the rainbow trout, though the rainbow's wild ancestor is the formidable steelhead. Large reservoirs such as Bewl Water, Rutland Water or Grafham Water are stocked with both brown and rainbow trout, though it is the cheaper and more plentiful rainbows that make up the bulk of

LEFT The adipose fin of a rainbow trout indicates its game fish status

ABOVE Day ticket trout fisheries can offer terrific sport

more room to enjoy the terrific sport that is available.

The big reservoirs offer a chance to fish for acclimatised fish, which were stocked at 2 lb but have doubled in size on a natural diet and regrown their raggedy fins and tails, taking on a magnificent silvery sheen. If it is sheer size that you want, though, many smaller water stock fish of well over double figures, and some can be stalked, using weighted flies, where the water clarity allows. Different strains of rainbow trout have been developed, such as golden trout and blue trout and hybrids such as cheetahs and tiger trout, using American brook trout.

But these are all fly-only waters, and we should not be snobbish about how we fish for trout, since they can be caught in many ways, such as with spinners or worms suspended under a bubble float or trotted down a stream.

Though salmon may be kings, trout are princes among fish and well worthy of our attention, being as they are wily adversaries, game fighters and magnificent eating when cooked outside on an open fire with nothing more than a nub of butter and a squeeze of lemon.

catches. The boom in stillwater trout fishing in the 1970s and '80s brought trout fishing within the budget of the average person for the first time. The novelty of eating freshly caught trout for a ticket costing a fiver meant banks were lined when the season opened at the start of April each year.

These days there are many more put-and-take trout fisheries of all sizes, but this merely means there is

Uptide & Unhooking

UPTIDE ANGLING FROM A BOAT IS a sea fishing technique that involves casting your bait against the running tide from an anchored craft in depths usually less than 30 metres. The idea is to get the bait away from the boat to avoid the disturbance caused by the tide on the hull and anchor chain, known as the scare area.

Uptide rods are different from ordinary boat rods in that they are lighter and punchier, which helps get the bait to a position on the uptide side of the boat where the wire grips of a Breakaway lead can pin the bait to the sandy or gravelly sea bed.

The angler lets off slack line, which runs downtide, and so the bait - a nice juicy sandeel - sits on the sea bed waiting to be found. Bottom-feeding fish such as a thornback ray or dogfish pick up the bait and move off with it undis-

turbed by any resistance from the slack line, while the angler spots the movement on the rod tip. He reels in the slack line, feels the fish on the end and sets the hook.

ABOVE Uptide rods are lighter and punchier than standard boat rods

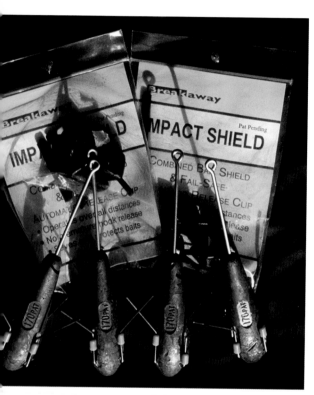

ABOVE The wire grips of a Breakaway lead will hold a bait still in the tide

1970s in the Thames estuary, when Essex lads reaped a rich harvest over the shallow waters fishing from small charter boats. Tope were among their main quarry, but uptiders can also expect to catch cod, bass and smoothhound.

Rods tend to be up to 9 ft in length and reels small and loaded with light line, but most important is a fast retrieve, to take up the slack quickly prior to the strike. Often the fish will lift the lead from the sea bed and carry it down towards the boat, meaning even more frantic reeling-in.

Rigs are usually single-hook or two hooks tied Pennel-style in tandem to take a big bait, with a short paternoster or a running trace. Fixed-wire leads can be used as well as Breakaway leads, and I recommend you hang the baited hook from one of the wires to shorten the length of the rig when casting.

And always remember that casting from a boat is hazardous and calls for extra vigilance. Let people around you know you are about to cast, and have your rig outside of the boat as you do so, taking care to avoid any protrusions such as masts or radar aerials.

Uptiding differs from wreck fishing, which is done with a traditional boat

Uptiding works particularly well in a strong tide, and is one of the most consistently successful techniques employed by sea anglers, with a dedicated following. It gained popularity during the

rubber eels lowered close enough to the wreck to find them.

Alternatively, anchor uptide and drop your whole mackerel or squid-tipped pirk into the wreck, knowing that you may suffer heavy tackle losses but also get among the biggest fish, including a big ling or a conger eel.

Much of sea fishing is governed by tides, which ebb and flow twice a day and strongly affect the movement and behaviour of fish. Every two weeks or so, when the moon is in line with the earth, spring tides occur, causing the highest tides and most disturbance to the sea bed. Bottom feeding fish will come close inshore in the roughest weather to scavenge for worms, crabs and sandeels thrown up by the action of the water.

It's worth being on the beach for the spring and autumn equinox tides (March 21 and September 23). As well as rising to the highest level of the year,

LEFT Efficient unhooking demands the right tools for the job

BELOW A giant bass caught uptiding in California

rod, made short and powerful to lower heavy weights below baited hooks downtide or uptide of wrecks or over them as you drift past. The UK's seas are littered with shipwrecks, and most are recorded on nautical charts, allowing charter skippers to find them and log their position with GPS satellite tracking, to return again with ease.

Wrecks are home to large concentrations of fish, which live in and around them, feeding on the smaller fish that find shelter there. Cod, pollack, bass, coalfish, ling and conger eels all inhabit the rusting, rotting hulks, and often these will take lures such as pirks or

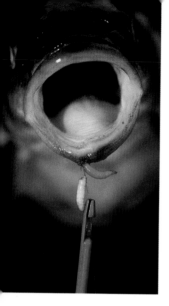

. **ABOVE** Disgorgers are cheap and invaluable for popping out hooks

they also fall to the lowest levels, which is a good time to gather bait and look for flounders lying on sandbanks.

But remember to respect the sea at all times, whether you are on a mud flat, where you could be cut off by the tide, or a rocky ledge, where a rough wave could sweep you in. Wear a lifejacket or a flotation suit – the investment could be the best decision of your life.

Unhooking

UNHOOKING YOUR CATCH QUICKLY and efficiently is the sign of a skilled and considerate angler, and comes about through a combination of correct technique and the right tools for the job. No matter how careful we are, there will always be times when a pike takes a bait further back than we would have wished, or when a carp gets a hook embedded in a tough part of its mouth.

All pleasure anglers and match anglers should carry disgorgers, which are inexpensive and invaluable for popping out hooks that are out of sight or accessible but reluctant to budge. They come in several sizes, to take hooks of up to specimen hunting dimensions, and can be tied on a cord and looped around your neck, with spare ones kept in your box.

Pike anglers should carry at least one pair of artery forceps, and ideally a gardening glove and a pair of wire cutters, in case you hook yourself or the pike rolls in the net and snags the mesh with loose trebles.

To unhook them efficiently, lie them on their back on an unhooking mat (another essential for big-fish anglers) and kneel astride the fish, holding it with your fingers inside the gill flap under its chin. The jaws should drop open, and you will have a good view of what you are doing.

Carp anglers now carry small bottles of anti-bacterial gel to smear on hook holes and any abrasions spotted on a fish's body. Taking the trouble to care for your catch in this way is not only providing yourself and others with better sport in the future, but also shows the non-angling public that anglers have the interests of the fish they catch at heart.

Venables &
Very large fish

VENABLES IS A NAME WITH STRONG literary links to angling, from 15th Century scribe Robert Venables pronouncing on various matters piscatorial in The Experienced Angler, to Bernard Venables, 20th Century creator of the inspirational comic-style series featuring Mr Crabtree.

Angling has had a long and highly fruitful association with literature, with a vast number of books written about it, from technical tomes extolling various techniques, to scientific analysis of fish habitats, and grand stories of fact and fiction. Everyone from Aelfric the Abbot to William Shakespeare have dipped their quill in angling's name, and Izaak Walton admitted "I love any

LEFT Bernard Venables, creator of the inspirational comic-style angling series Mr Crabtree Goes Fishing

RIGHT Today's angling literature is poured out in publications like Angler's Mail

discourse on rivers, and fish and fishing". And so say all of us.

One of the earliest writers, Dame Juliana Berners in Treatyse of Fysshynge wyth an Angle (1496), emphasised the need not to over commercialise angling to the detriment of future sport, while others wrote that we should try to increase our understanding of fish, and in so doing add to our appreciation of them.

Frank Buckland published A Log Book of a Fisherman and Zoologist in 1873, joining Cholmondeley-Pennell's The Angler Naturalist (1868) on the book shelves. Dry-fly purists Skues and Halford studied the natural fly in great detail and brought out Floating Flies and How to Dress Them (1886) and Minor Tactics of the Chalkstream (1910).

Some writers have changed accepted thinking on a topic, and when George Bainbridge published The Fly-fisher's Guide in 1816 he convinced people that salmon fishing could be practised as a specialised form of angling. Mr Nobbles had already covered the subject of trolling in The Compleate Troller, in 1682, while H. Sheringham offered a new approach to his subject in Coarse Fishing in 1913.

RIGHT Today's angling literature is poured out in publications like Angler's Mail

Arthur Ransome, Ernest Hemingway and John Buchan have all put pen to paper in praise of angling, while Francis Francis was the angling correspondent for The Field in the 17th Century and felt it was important to be inclusive of all types of angling. His memory lives on in the form of an active club, Francis

Francis AC, who meet and fish on the Thames at Twickenham, mooring their traditional punts in front of their waterside headquarters The Barmy Arms, which is lined with old pictures and memorabilia.

Richard Walker was a legend in his own lifetime and that rare combination of scientist, inventor, naturalist and wonderfully clear and lucid writer willing and able to challenge conventional thinking, as well as a first-class angler. Many of the techniques and tackle items used today are based on his designs, and even now, 20 years after his death, he is still spoken of in tones of great respect by all whose lives were touched by his words.

Dick Walker gained as much of a following from his weekly angling newspaper column and magazine writing as he did from his many books, and today's angling literature is poured out most readily in the wide range of angling periodicals available from the newsagent's. Such writers as sea angler Mike Thrussell and all-rounder Andy Little in Angler's Mail seek to draw people into their world of a thoughtful, considered approach to angling, which leads to better catches and a greater enjoyment.

Without angling writers the sport would be a much poorer place, for what is the point of a memorable experience if it cannot be shared with others of a similar interest? When we cannot be at the water, reading about others' adventures will always come a close second.

ABOVE The 17th Century angling writer Francis Francis

Very large fish

VERY BIG FISH HAVE ALWAYS
occupied the thoughts and dreams of
anglers, but there has never been a better time to tangle with something truly
colossal. The world is opening up to
angling possibilities, and holiday companies specialising in fishing are taking anglers with the travelling urge to
far-flung places to battle with fish of
unimaginable size.

If you always dreamed of donning a
harness and climbing into a fighting
chair to trail a lure with a hook the size
of your hand behind a boat and watch
the reel smoke as you play something
twice your size for several hours,
Ernest Hemingway-style, now is the
time to do it.

Carp of 60 lb are readily available in
France, catfish of 200 lb in Spain, huge
coho salmon in Canada, outsize sturgeon in Russia, massive mahseer in
India, giant Nile perch in Egypt, as well
as big game species such as marlin, tarpon, tunny and sailfish, and a whole
variety of sharks, up to and including
the great white.

Even the UK is getting in on the act,
with tuna of 900 lb being landed off the
coast of Ireland by anglers targeting fish
widely considered to be among the
biggest of their species in the world,
brought there on the Gulf Stream. And

huge halibut are still winched up off the Scottish coast by those who know where to find them.

Companies like Anglers World Holidays, in Chesterfield (Tel: 01246 221717), are a good place to start, or European Catfish Trips, in Denham, (Tel: 01895 835745), who will try to help you catch a 100 lb-plus catfish from Spain's River Ebro. A couple of Britain's best anglers have turned to guiding, and take parties of anglers on package deals to realise their dreams in Florida or India.

The newest destination is the Far East, where species unseen before by western anglers grow to arm-aching proportions in Thailand. Often on these type of trips the tackle and bait is provided, and all you need to do is strap yourself in and when the chance arises hang on for dear life and the thrill of a lifetime.

But we cannot leave the subject of very big fish without making a mention of the British rod-caught salmon record, and doffing our collective caps to Miss Georgina Ballantine. While being rowed in a boat on the River Tay by her gillie on October 7, 1922, Miss B felt a tug on her line and then spent the

next two hours playing and boating the largest salmon ever caught in Britain, at 64 lb, a feat that left her arm swollen for two weeks after.

A fish of that size today on modern tackle would test the skill and nerve of any man, but on heavy, primitive equipment in the hands of a lady angler it constitutes a truly outstanding feat of angling, and a fish the like of which we will probably never see again from these shores.

ABOVE This 1,014 lb mako shark was caught by English angler Leo Kennedy

Wading & Wrasse

ABOVE Wading will take you closer to the fish and reduce the size of your silhouette on the horizon

WADING IS A DANGEROUS ACTIVITY not to be undertaken lightly or wantonly. The desire to get closer to one's quarry can be intense, and lead to all kinds of problems and mishaps. The benefits include being able to fish further out, and reducing the size of your silhouette on the horizon, but the perils include a soaking or worse.

Coarse anglers are fairly sensible about staying on terra firma, and are more likely to sit on a box or chair on the bank or in the shallows, though trotting can call for a better vantage point. But trout and salmon angling goes hand-in-hand with wading, often up to one's chest in a powerful river with boulders bigger than footballs to negotiate.

Victorian salmon anglers advised others not to go beyond the fifth button of their waistcoat (no doubt so as not to wet their tie), and to pay attention to the colour of their legs when wading in February. Ruddy legs were fine, but black or purple legs meant it was time to get out of the water.

No need for bare legs these days, as there are rubber waders available fairly

Spey. A flotation jacket is also a worth-while purchase, in case your worst fears are realised and you get a soaking.

When wading a river never cross your legs, keep sideways to the current and probe ahead of you with your wading stick. If you do feel the gravel slip away from under you, keep calm, shut your mouth, and put your feet up. The current will carry you down-stream like so much flotsam, and deliver you on to a shallow beach, where you can crawl ashore.

Always peer into the water before you step in to wade, in case a fish is lying in the edge and can be covered before you disturb the water. And remember never to wear waders in boats. If you go over-board they will fill up with water and take you to the bottom like a pair of concrete boots.

Carried out safely, wading can add another dimension to your sport, as well as being the coolest place to be on a hot summer's day. There is nothing like standing in the warm margins of a reservoir as the sun goes down sur-rounded by rising fish and covered in newly hatched flies to renew one's won-der at the stunning beauty and rich diversity of the natural world.

LEFT Rubber waders are not expensive and could add a new dimension to your fishing

cheaply, and neoprene waders which insulate the angler from the cold for those with a little more to spend.

A wading stick is a necessary accessory when fishing a powerful river like the

ABOVE Neoprene waders insulate you from the cold for a little more money

OPPOSITE Wrasse like this 4 lb 10 oz ballan are the chameleons of the sea world

Wrasse

WRASSE ARE THE CHAMELEONS of the seas – a family of attractive fish that can adapt their colour to match the surroundings of the world they inhabit.

The wildly colourful cuckoo wrasse is brilliant blue-backed and gold-flanked in the male and a vivid pink and black spotted in the female.

They are found off the southern English coasts, though how this colour reflects the English Channel only they know. Ballan wrasse are more common, and slightly less extrovert in their livery of dark green with gold spotted flanks.

But it is the lips of wrasse that take you aback. Many a film starlet would swap mouths with these bee-strung beauties. However, beneath the rubbery protrusions lie bright white peg-teeth designed for tearing limpets and barnacles from rocks, and getting their own back on unwary anglers.

Wrasse have a further set of pharyngeal teeth set back in their throat, to grind up the molluscs into digestible pieces. They live along deep, rocky coasts, where exciting fishing can be had with one of their favourite baits - peeler crab.

These are crabs at the stage when they are going through their annual change of shell, shedding the old one and growing a new one, and fish know they make a tasty morsel with little in the way of protection until their new shell has hardened.

The crabs hide under rocks and seaweed in their soft-backed state, which is where anglers collect them at low tide. Lever them out and thread them on a hook, binding them in place with cotton to make an irresistible bait for wrasse and lots of other species, too.

A paternoster rig with a rotten bottom (a lighter line to the lead, to snap off when it gets snagged) is the best way to approach them. Lower this down into their watery world, where the wrasse will be swaying in the eddy of the waves among the strands of bright seaweed, searching for food among the rocks.

You will want your bait to be about eight inches above the sea bed, and then wait for those first exploratory tugs, followed by an explosion of power.

Wrasse are hard fighters, and when they realise they have been hooked will storm the stage and dive for the nearest rocks. It is up to you to keep them out or risk losing your prize. Set the clutch on your reel in advance to just short of breaking point, and show them who's boss.

Tackle losses could be heavy, so instead of using leads bring plenty of old nuts and bolts to tie on your line. So long as you are not casting while using a rotten bottom rig, but just lowering your bait down, there is no risk of the weight snapping off and picking off a passer-by as if he has been shot.

You can even floatfish for them if you want to avoid hooking the bottom. Plumb the depth with a weight heavy enough to take the float under if you are set too shallow, and then take the weight off, shallow up a few inches and present your offering.

But while watching the float, keep your eyes on the waves. One moment the sea may be lapping at your feet and then the next swamping you with a ton of water. The sea has a way of dealing with the unwary, and can be an unpredictable companion. Like a mischievous friend, turn your back on it at your peril.

RIGHT Wrasse have a formidable set of teeth for dealing with limpets and barnacles

Xenocrates

XENOCRATES WAS A GREEK philosopher who had a deep love of fish, in particular on his plate. First he would dissect them, to see what they were about, and then he would eat them. As the founder of descriptive biology as we know it, he was engaged in ground-breaking work, but enjoying himself with the leftovers.

He was a student of Plato, and worked alongside another high flier, Aristotle, and most Greeks realised the medicinal and culinary benefits of fish. Xenocrates once said as he polished off the remains of one of his specimens "the tail end of all fishes is the most wholesome part, on account of its being most frequently exercised".

A love of eating fish and of fishing is not unusual. One of this country's finest chefs, Marco Pierre White, is a keen angler, and when he is not running his collection of stylish West End restaurants you may find him rod in hand beside the Hampshire Avon angling for pike and barbel.

LEFT Famous chef Marco Pierre White is a keen angler, with fish like this 30 lb Pike to his credit

ABOVE Oily fish like trout contain healthy omega-3 fatty acids

We are told that we should be eating at least three portions of oily fish every week, and that sprats, mackerel, herring, trout, salmon, tuna and sardines are all very good for us because of the omega-3 fatty acids they contain.

As well as contributing to good health through brain and nerve tissue development in children, and healthier skin and eyes in adults, oily fish is said to protect the body against heart disease. I've always suspected that raw cod liver oil out of the bottle was good for me because it tasted so disgusting.

The human body is able to utilise fish protein faster and more efficiently than meat or dairy protein, which are made of saturated fats, compared to the unsaturated fats of fish. Unsaturated fats are less viscous than saturated fats, which is why they are found in fish, which live in a cold environment, where saturated fats would congeal.

Omega-3 fatty acids in unsaturated fats cannot be manufactured by humans, so fish have a vital role to play in our long-term health, and we have a duty to maintain sustainable fish populations of both wild and farmed stocks for the good of our own future.

Wild salmon numbers have suffered due to demand for their flesh by consumers, which once led to the netting of river mouths and drift nets along the coast, reducing stocks of migrating fish. The removal of these nets was as a result of angler pressure, but also aided by the increasing availability of much cheaper farmed salmon.

This seemed, at the time, to be the perfect answer, and was embraced like a long-lost friend. Science enabled us to create artificial environments suitable for the farming of species such as halibut, turbot, cod, trout, salmon, plaice and bass. But now there are legitimate concerns about the impact these are having on the natural environment, from the point of view of disease, pollution and the dilution of the natural populations with farmed escapees. A balance will have to be sought if more damage is not to be done to the natural world by our efforts to harness it to our own ends.

Catch and release is now common practise on salmon rivers in a way that would have been unthinkable 20 years ago, but to wish to take home a fish for the pot is a primitive and understandable desire. To fish and to eat what we catch is a basic, primeval instinct, and one that knew almost no bounds in previous centuries, when we were less finicky in our tastes.

BELOW Sea fish gastronomes rate John Dory as the finest eating fish

ABOVE Maybe we would all be happier if we ate more fish

(with a dozen oysters) and baked sturgeon. Speaking personally, give me a brown trout or a mackerel cooked on a camping stove within minutes of being caught, but people took their protein however and wherever they could get it in those days, and were glad to do so.

Perhaps we shall come full circle and have to learn to be less choosy about what fish we eat. When cod are no more than a memory, and haddock found only in the pages of science and history books, perhaps we will return to our former dishes like old friends, or find ourselves ordering half a kilo of hoki for our fish supper.

In 1890 Mrs Beeton, (the Delia Smith of her day) had many a fine recipe for barbel ("with a fagot of sweet herbs"), crimped skate, stewed carp, boiled eels, fried flounders, perch stewed in wine, boiled pike, matelot of tench

Maybe anglers will be seen in a different light, then, like butchers during war-time rationing – favoured individuals sought out and cultivated by members of the community in the hope that some of the fruits of their profession might come their way.

For what it's worth, I believe that one of the finest health benefits of fish is in the pursuit of them. It has been argued that an angler expends as much energy in the course of a day's fishing as players of more active sports. Apparently the constant casting of fly fishing, the regular unshipping involved in pole fishing and the carrying of vast amounts of heavy tackle to the waterside all get our hearts pumping to a healthy degree, not to mention the excitement of success.

Combine this with the soothing effect of being beside the water in a natural environment, and the benefits of fresh air, and you can see why anglers often live long lives and enjoy rude health.

If you also eat more fish than most as an angler, due to its availability, the sport could be seen as a lifestyle choice for the health conscious, advised to take up fishing on their doctor's orders.

These reflect a different level of health benefits from angling, starting with the preparation of equipment and bait, to the setting up of the rod and tying of the hook on the line and the casting of a line. This will see frowns of minor importance replaced with furrows of concentration and very soon, you will have relaxed and recharged the batteries and be feeling better already.

BELOW Pack a stove and cook mackerel within minutes of capture for a meal that takes some beating

Yolk Sac

YOLK SACS ARE BASICALLY overnight bags of unconsumed nutrients left over from the egg stage that newly hatched fish carry around with them. They hang from their throat, enabling them to remain self sufficient for a number of days.

BELOW Tench wait for warm weather before laying up to 800,000 eggs

Just how much yolk is in each sac varies not only from species to species, but also with the temperature, less energy being needed in warm conditions. A large tench in the warm, still waters of a pond in June may lay up to 800,000 eggs, each one being 1.2 mm in diameter, and these will stick to weed at the bottom of the pond. Carp and bream fry also have adhesive organs, so that they can attach themselves to plants when being buffeted by the water.

These tench eggs contain very little yolk and develop fast, hatching after a few days into very small alevins, which quickly use up their tiny sac and then become fry and have to seek their own food.

Being only 2.5 mm in length they can feed only on minute organisms such as rotifers and water fleas. The going is tough, and out of the 800,000 eggs laid, only about eight tench will reach mature breeding size at four years old.

The rate at which they grow is dependent on the size of the egg, and as different species have different sizes of eggs, they also have different growth rates. The time at which each species lays its eggs also varies from species to species, each requiring a certain water

water spawnings of coarse fish. A salmon egg may be 6 mm in diameter, but they lay only around 6,000, delivered to fall into a depression in the gravel prepared with her tail, known as a redd.

The alevin will hatch with a large yolk sac attached to it, and live among the gravel for up to six weeks relying entirely on its sac of goodies. By this time it should be a fry of 24 mm in length, ready to face the full current of the stream and dodge waiting predators.

Meanwhile in the dark depth of the Atlantic, cod will be moving towards inshore waters in the spring to spawn at depths of up to 300 feet. The adult cod that have been inhabiting inshore waters during the winter will move offshore to reproduce, where the chances of the survival of the eggs is greater without the attentions of other hungry species.

Unlike other fish, cod are known as 'batch-spawners' which means that the female may release up to 20 batches of eggs at intervals of 60 hours, with each batch containing several hundred thousand eggs. Only a very small number need to reach maturity for the population to remain stable.

All freshwater fish eggs are heavier then water, though some have special

temperature to be reached before they can spawn.

In the cooler waters of a slow-moving river in early April we will find a slightly larger egg being laid. A 10 lb pike will lay maybe 100,000 eggs of 3 mm in diameter. These take a little longer to hatch and the resultant alevin's yolk sac is slightly larger, to allow it to depend on the nutrients until it is about 6 mm in length and tough enough to find food for itself.

Salmon and sea-trout spawn in January in the cold, fast water of upland streams, and their eggs are positively huge in comparison with the warmer

LEFT Stripping eggs from a brown trout at a West Country hatchery

BELOW Milt from a cock fish makes them fertile

attachment mechanisms to secure them to tree roots and weed. But Atlantic cod eggs are free floating and drift on the currents in clouds until they hatch, the length of time taken being dependent upon the temperature.

Whiting and haddock eggs also just drift with the ocean currents, but their larvae live beneath large jellyfish, hiding among the stinging tentacles, which they use as protection against predators.

On hatching, the young codling have grown from eggs of 1 mm in diameter to 4 mm in length and are known as larvae rather than alevins. Their yolk sacs last for about a week, and then the larvae begin to feed on vegetable matter know as phytoplankton, drifting animal life called zooplankton and then krill, tiny free-float shrimps. This is a menu shared with some of the biggest creatures on earth, namely whales, along with almost every other fish in the sea.

After about three weeks of hardship the larvae that have managed to find enough zooplankton to survive become recognisable for the first time, as tiny transparent juvenile cod. They move to the bottom of the sea to live and feed and hide from predators, which include their own parents, parenthood carrying no particular responsibilities in the world of fishes. Soon their mouth will grow big enough to keep pace with their appetite, and they will become of interest to us, armed with rod and line.

Temperature is a crucial element in spawning, sexual maturity and growth rate. Plaice lay up to half a million eggs, which float at first and then sink to the bottom, depending on temperature.

The colder the water, the longer it takes for the fish to mature, and cold water fish, some of which have developed an antifreeze protein to stop themselves icing up, take longest to mature.

This has major ramifications for the future of fish stocks and the effects of commercial fishing. Cold water species are more easily damaged and take longer to recover than warm water ones, so the harm done to cod and salmon numbers is felt more keenly, and if continued is less likely to recover.

Also, commercial size limits on catches allow fish to be taken over a length of around 12 inches. This is close to the size at which many fish mature and first become able to breed and reproduce, so if at that moment they are scooped up and turned into fishcakes, the future for the species looks grim.

LEFT Alevins carry their food in the form of a yolk sac hanging from their throat

Zander & Zulu

CENTRE Perch are colourful characters in more ways than one

BELOW Zander can grow to over 20 lb, and have a dedicated following among specimen hunters

ZANDER ARE THE WOLVES OF THE coarse fish world. Voracious predators that hunt in packs, they also have a pair of tiny 'fangs' at the front of their upper jaw, which make tell-tale double puncture marks on baits they mouth, as if they have been bitten by a vampire.

Despised by matchmen for their appetite for small fish but sought out by specimen hunters for their size and bristling beauty, they were introduced to the UK in 1878 at Woburn Lakes, in Bedfordshire. The intention was to keep them in land-locked waters, but they spread into the Great Ouse river system and from there into the Fen drains, where they found the population of small fish greatly to their liking.

How they then turned up in rivers on the other side of England such as the Warwickshire Avon and the River Severn, the latter producing a former British record fish of 18 lb 10 oz, is a matter for speculation. Many blame anglers for their spread, but no one has

ever been brought to book.

The result is that zander are just about everywhere in England, having to be netted out of canals because they are overpopulating areas, and appearing in trout fishery Grafham Water, supposedly from eggs pumped in with top-up water from local rivers.

Also known as pike-perch, due to their similarities to both species, they are a true species and not a hybrid of the two. They are widespread throughout Europe, where anglers tend to spin for them, but in England a scaled-down version of pike-fishing, with small freshwater fish for bait, is employed

Night time is often the best, particularly if the days are bright, as zander have excellent night vision, and their eyes glow like a cat's in the glare of a torch or a camera flash.

If you are intent on catching one, two stillwaters where they are stocked offer the best chance, namely Bury Hill Lake, near Dorking, in Surrey, and Coombe Abbey Lake, near Coventry, in Warwickshire, both of which have produced fish to over double figures.

Perch have big mouths and even bigger appetites. Young perch will gobble anything that comes their way, and put away more maggots than you would have though possible or prudent for such a small fish, while the adults see nothing wrong in consuming their own young.

Spinning will catch them, particularly if a hank of red wool is tied to the treble hook, though the perch that grabs your lure may be smaller than the lure itself.

They are a shoal fish which like to use obstructions in the water, such as tree roots and fence posts to ambush their prey, which is usually a roach fry, a bleak or a minnow,

BELOW The pope, or daddy ruffe, is another member of the perch family, along with zander

though they are particularly partial to gudgeon.

Worms will also catch them, especially lobworm tails, but however you fish for them you must reduce any resistance to the taking fish to nothing, or perch of worthwhile size will drop the bait in a second.

A 4 lb perch is a very big fish, and one of 2 lb an impressive capture, with its bright red fins and prickly dorsal fin. Watch out for the spike on its gill cover when unhooking one, as it is razor sharp.

Ruffe also bear the nickname of 'pope' and resemble a small perch in all but colouration. They are found in rivers, lakes and canals around Britain, and enjoyed a mini population explosion in Scotland a few years ago when English anglers took them north to use as livebaits and they gained an unnatural foothold.

Ruffe are appreciated by match anglers for their ability to feed when other fish shut up shop, and are also said to be popular with gastronomes for their firm and sweet flesh, despite their tiny size.

Zulu

ZULU IS A TRADITIONAL PATTERN of wet fly used for catching brown trout, sea-trout and rainbows, and its attraction may lie in its use of colours seen most clearly by fish. Experiments by scientists at Stirling University some years ago concluded that the eye of a trout sees black and red more starkly than other hues, suggesting the Zulu and flies such as the Peter Ross, with its barred wing and red front body, should outscore others. However theory and practise are often reluctant bedfellows.

The Zulu is a traditional pattern tied with cock hackles palmered along its body over a layer of seal's fur to create an illusion of legs and wings beating furiously as the imitation insect struggles to break through the choppy surface of the water.

It comes into its own when fished on Scottish and Irish trout waters and cast in front of a boat drifting side-on down the wind. It often occupies the middle dropper of a team of three flies drawn through the waves and lifted with the rod to make them seem as if they are about to take off and escape.

It also makes a fine sea-trout fly on Scottish, Irish and Welsh rivers, as with the addition of a silver rib of flat tinsel to protect it from the sharp teeth of trout it has the flash of a small fish.

Whether trout take flies because they are close imitations of insects or fish or because they are intrigued or annoyed by this darting upstart is another area of debate. Certainly, trout have been caught on some strange, garish patterns the like of which has never been seen among the ranks of insects and fish fry.

And anglers cleaning their catch at the end of the day have come across the sort of strange objects in the stomach of fish that make one wonder if we are wasting our time matching the hatch.

But at other times trout will ignore everything except one pattern tied in one size, to the frustration of the angler who loses his last one and throws everything else in the box at them to no avail.

That is the joy and the frustration of angling – the never-ending quest for answers, the small victories, the puzzling set-backs and the eternal optimism. They keep us coming back for more, and long may it continue.

LEFT Why do trout take the flies that we offer them?

Bibliograpy
Sea Trout Fishing - Hugh Falkus
Stillwater Trout Flies - Robson's guide
Rivers and Lochs of Scotland - Bruce Sanderson
Salmon fishing - Lonsdale Library
Distant waters - Nick Lyons/Val Atkinson

Anglers Fishes - Their Natural History - Lonsdale Library
Fish, Fishing and The Meaning of Life - Jeremy Paxman
The Fisherman's Vade Mecum - G W Maunsell
Freshwater Fishing - Fred Buller and Hugh Falkus
Trawler - Redmond 0'hanlon
The Book of Household Management - Mrs Beeton

Guide to Salt Water Fishing - Martin Ford
Cod - Mark Kurlansky
Sea Fishing - Ian Ball
An Introduction to Sea Fishing - Trevor Housby

The pictures in this book were provided courtesy of the following:

ANGLER'S MAIL MAGAZINE
IPC, King's Reach Tower, Stamford Street, London SE1 9LS

THE FIELD MAGAZINE,
IPC, King's Reach Tower, Stamford Street, London SE1 9LS

GETTY IMAGES
101 Bayham Street, London NW1 0AG

Book design and artwork by Nicole Saward, Green Umbrella
Based on a design by Darren Roberts

Published by Green Umbrella

Series Editors Jules Gammond and Vanessa Gardner

Written by Rob Yorke with Greg Meenehan

Special thanks to Tim Knight, editor Angler's Mail and Emma Parkin.
Thanks to Chris Yates, Rob Yorke and Dave Houghton for providing their pictures.
Inside cover photograph of Rob Yorke courtesy of Discovery Home and Leisure.